Host or
HOSTAGE?

A Guide for Surviving House Guests

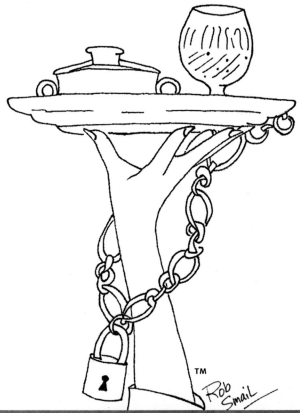

ILLUSTRATED BY ROBERT SMAIL   EDITED BY DIANNE KERNELL

Darlene Dennis

A BARTHUR HOUSE BOOK

HOST OR HOSTAGE?
A Guide for Surviving Houseguests
by Darlene Dennis

Illustrations by Robert Smail
Edited by Diane Kernell

Host or Hostage © 2008 by Darlene Dennis
www.HostOrHostage.com
darlenedennis@hostorhostage.com

Soft Cover ISBN: 1-933428-48-1
Hard Cover ISBN: 1-933428-86-4
Library of Congress number pending.

Layout, Design and Publication Management by:
Lamp Post Inc.
619.589.1400
www.lamppostpubs.com

BARTHUR HOUSE PUBLISHING
ENCINITAS, CA

To Arthur, my patient, kind, generous, loving husband who has been instrumental in bringing this project to fruition.

Table of Contents

Acknowledgements

Without the encouragement, ideas proofreading, editorial advice and helpful hints from great friends this book would have continued to lie dormant in my mind.

My superb editor, Dianne Kernell is without equal on the planet. Her expertise in analyzing, proofreading and suggesting are equal only to her skillful diplomacy and patience.

My husband, Arthur Bauer made his insomnia work for me and did his own version of slash and burn during his line editing.

Thanks to Shannon Smail for introducing me to her brother, Robert Smail, an extremely talented cartoonist, who agreed on short notice to produce the illustrations specifically for this book. I'm certain his creations help us to better understand the many facets of entertaining house guests and visualize incidents with a smile. Dick Donaldson assisted Robert by supplying suggestions for some of the details in the pictures.

Nancy Clifford critiqued an early draft with her journalist's eye and she is also an excellent photographer. She snapped the picture with Foxy which appears on the back cover.

Though I have changed names (including my own) to protect the polite and the impolite, I do want to thank those who contributed to this effort.

I've interviewed people anywhere and everywhere, "Have you ever had any interesting house guest experiences?" Just when I think I've heard it all, a story to top the others pops up. What fun! I owe a load of thanks to the following contributors and many more whose names I failed — or forgot to put on my list.

Teresa Whittaker, Lynn Payette and Dr. Robbi Simons reign as my indefatigable needle women. They needled me mercilessly to launch and complete this project. Martha Mc Donald, my heroine, mentor, guide and sorority sister from the University of Southern Mississippi politely concealed her revulsion upon dutifully reading the embryonic drafts of this work.

Grateful thanks go to the following friends and acquaintances who provided anecdotal material to exemplify my views: Joyce Bressler, Gayle Carroll, Carol Cruger, Barbara Galey, Sharon Gher, Rose Going, Marla Jensen, Jane Woulfe and Una Yakatan — my Mah Jongg buddies — who regaled me with their stories while beating me with their jokers.

The Nutter family contributed several stories; they are Sue and Hugh, Nick and Kathy, Jay and Barbara as well as Nancy and Dave from Sorrento Valley Automotive.

Sally Billig provided one of the very best anecdotes, though she assures me that she has never had a bad house guest experience. My lunch buddy, Merry Terry provided her slant for a couple of stories.

The aqua exercise classes at the Magdalena Eke YMCA proved to be my very best resource library. Where else could a novice author have so much fun and (sort of) keep her body in shape while gathering material for a book? My contributing laugh and splash friends are: Jean Allen, Ginny Brill, Teresa Caesar, Barbara Charos, Al Crane, Aruna Durbin, Anne Fobes, Ellen Falk, Lynn Perry Garland, Marie Gaskowicz, Kari Gjerde, Joan Greiser, Joy Hamer, Geri Hohen, Claire Johnson, Angie Raimo, Roxanne Hays, Laverne Jones, Sue Kasche, Dianne Kernell, Karen Lai, Ann Larsen, Russ McCormick, Jan

McMackin, Jill Rogul, Candice Young-Schult and Tanna Tonnu, as well as Bonnie, Angie, Eve, Neme, Alex, Phil, and Charlene whose last names I don't know, but all of whom added stories, tidbits and ideas along with laughs that helped bring this to fruition.

Friends from American Association of University Women: Karen Delinger, Karen and Ken Gallagher, Jackie De Walt Mason, Lillian Lachicotte, provided a number of anecdotal stories.

Joannie and Bernie Goott, Hermina Saluup, Vonne Phoummaseng, Marie Calahan, Gordon Dooley, Susan Lauer and, Margaret Davies also supplied their fair share of anecdotal material.

My friend from high school, Carolyn Morton, gave me a couple of stories as did my college friend, JoAnn Denley.

Margot and Clifford Shupp, along with several other lovely people that I met during Elderhostel tours and adventure trips abroad with Overseas Adventure Travel.

My friends and neighbors, Anita Lewis, Annette White, Betty Plattner added a couple of stories from their rich histories of entertaining as did my dear friends Yasmin Hamud, and Jane Tatum .

Cynthia Henk entertained me with her houseguest from hell story while she cleaned my teeth. Sydney LeBlanc provided two stories during a spontaneous meeting in the Albertson parking lot.

Nancy Appleton, nutritionist author took a Sunday morning to advise me on some of the in's and out's of publishing.

Of course, I want to especially thank "Boorish Bob" and those many boundary breaking house guests who can't be named (for fear of reprisal, offending and even being sued). Without them there would be no good stories.

one

THE TROUBLE WITH HOUSEGUESTS (THE ENEMY IS US)

When you live in the country everybody is your neighbor
On this one thing you can rely
They'll all come to see you and they'll never ever leave you
Y'all come to see us bye and bye
Kinfolks a-comin', they're a-comin' by the dozen
Eating everything from soup to hay
And right after dinner, they ain't lookin' any thinner
And here's what you hear them say

Y'all come (y'all come), y'all come (y'all come)
Now Grandma's a-wishing you'd come out the kitchen
And help do the dishes right away
Then they all start a-leaving, and though she's a-grieving
You can still hear grandma say
Y'all come (y'all come), y'all come (y'all come)
Oh, you all come to see us when you can

"Y'All Come" by Arlie Duff 1953

After many years of entertaining, a bottom of the barrel "house guest from hell" experience finally convinced me that once more I had put myself in a position to be held hostage in my own home. Why was this happening to me? Here I am, a woman who loves the company of friends, old and new, a mother and wife who enjoys pampering and feeding loved ones. I should be the perfect hostess. Yet, time and again, my vision of a planned enjoyable weekend entertaining house guests has been shattered by the reality of people dropping by, unannounced and uninvited, planning to stay for "a few days." They proceed to eat my food ("No red meat, Darlene."), drive my car ("it's just a minor dent, Darlene."), and take over my life ("Darlene, your living room is so much nicer now that I've rearranged the furniture."). Instead of the happy hostess, I was the unhappy victim of my own chronic passive acceptance of over-reaching guests.

Arlie Duff's song, "Y'all Come," though written in 1953, might have been written for me. "Y'all come" humorously and ironically rhymes the contradictions inherent in hospitality customs around the world and especially here in the United States. The lyrics feature grandma held hostage by a sink full of dirty dishes. While grousing over the task, she's singing out her frustrations caused by the conflict of perception versus reality, "Y'all Come to see us when you can" after the guests—oblivious to her burden—have departed.

It wasn't until a particularly irritating house guest left my home that I finally stepped back and said, "What am I doing? Why would I allow anyone to invite himself to spend ten days at my house when I really didn't want company? Where did I learn this obsequious slavish behavior? Why didn't I speak up when a guest burnished his ego by grilling a polite fourteen year old non-athlete about the rules of soccer? Why did I wait for this guy who finally appeared an hour and a half after everyone else was ready for breakfast? Why didn't I speak up and stop the noisy political argument that spoiled a lovely dinner? Why didn't I tell this lush, who refused to eat strawberries because they were sprinkled with sugar, that the large amount of liquor he had drunk the night before was pure sugar?" The list of "bite my tongue" issues goes on interminably.

As I looked back at my past behavior, I realized I had a serious addiction. I could not say "NO" to entertaining a potential house guest, no matter how inconvenient, uncomfortable or expensive the visit might be. My social training had conspired with my ego, resulting in a people please dis-ease that can only be described as Advanced Doormat Syndrome (ADS) I was . . . I am . . . a Doormat. For decades, the problem had been building, and it had become severe. The enemy was not the house guest. The enemy was me. I had allowed myself to become a doormat, to be held hostage as a hostess.

Once I realized I was afflicted with the doormat syndrome, I wanted to know how others addressed the problems I faced. Looking through various books and newspapers offered little insight. Guidelines for the host and/or the guest may occasionally be found in newspaper columns and cartoons. Major books on etiquette may devote a page or two to the social décor expected when friends or family are invited to stay in a home for a few days. These are mainly useful for consultation about proper conduct at weddings, funerals, and formal dinner parties. But many of the real problems that surface with hosts and house guests have been largely ignored by the media.

Was I the only doormat in town, or were there others suffering from ADS? I began asking people if they had ever had a difficult or "interesting" house guest experience. Most people initially reacted by rolling their eyes, cringing, or laughing. Then they began unloading their stories.

Some harped on how their hospitality had been kicked in the shins by unconscionable takeover artists. Others regaled me with house guest antics about guests who were totally ignorant of the basic rules of etiquette. (They didn't know they didn't know or didn't seem to care they didn't know.) Hosts confessed they had been mired in family situations that demanded they don a plastic smile and entertain when they would rather not.

People from all around the United States and from a number of other countries told me countless "house guests from hell" experiences. Whether I was in a dentist's chair, the YMCA locker room, or an orchestra seat at the opera, my innocent question about house guests seemed to loose the tongue of whomever was present. It seems that almost everyone – from South Carolina to Somalia – is familiar with house guest visits gone wrong. As the numbers of stories grew, it became obvious that I was not the only one to be taken advantage of and held hostage by visitors. I was not suffering from a rare disorder. Far from it! Advanced Doormat Syndrome is an epidemic!

Of course, it always makes us feel better to learn that other people are making the same mistakes. Interviews revealed some people had an even worse case of ADS than I! At this point I knew I wanted to undergo some type of rehabilitation. I wanted to change my behavior so that I could count on experiencing the joy of having house guests and take pleasure in the experience every time. Before I could modify my behavior, I needed to identify the symptoms of the disease.

We are exceptionally friendly, warm, open, generous, and kind. We smile, we invite, we cook, clean, share, spend and give. My ADS surfaced when I invited a person to my home and found myself annoyed because this person overstepped so many social boundaries that I formerly thought everyone understood , respected and observed.

Until recently I have been guilty of willy-nilly extending a verbal invitation and then experiencing a mini-shock when the guest takes me up on it. If your social hyperbole in the form of "Y'all Come" or "Please Stay With Us Next Time You're in Town," is taken literally, it's time for you to analyze your actions. If you are cringing at the idea of entertaining and annoyed by having extended a verbal invitation in the first place, it's time for reflection. Did you move your mouth without engaging your brain?

Those few who insist they have never had a "bad" house guest encounter seem to have maintained firm limits and are gifted with the ability to think before opening their mouths to avoid offering spontaneous invitations.

Whether the visit is planned and initiated by the host or thought of and started by the guest, it is the host who makes that ultimate decision to entertain under his roof.

Snitching a line from President George W. Bush, the host is "The Decider." He is also "The Chooser." The host chooses whom he will entertain and then he decides for how long he will entertain the chosen. As the "decision-maker," the host is in charge of establishing the format for the visit, dates, time, menus and entertainment. If this is a genuine invitation, and if there is any sort of failure, the buck usually stops with the host. Those of us who are afflicted with ADS are hesitant to be the decider and to say "NO." We make the mistake of hosting the uninvited.

Trials and tribulations are on the horizon when all members of a family are not aware or in agreement concerning the responsibilities inherent in a pending visit by outsiders.

Before extending any invitation, it is absolutely necessary to consult other family members. This is the personal equivalent of enlisting an exploratory committee before throwing oneself into the race for president. More often than not, company disrupts the daily household routine. The inviter may blissfully entertain his special friend for a few days, but a life partner who wasn't included in the planning is apt to make the atmosphere mighty chilly when the visit is over.

A breakdown in communications surrounding who is invited and for how long, more often than not generates serious family friction. More than one person is afflicted with ADS if the uninformed partner/co-host quietly goes along with the program,

> *Recently a young woman with two small children told me she was upset because her husband had told her only two days before Thanksgiving that he had invited six of his family members to spend the holiday week with them in their small condominium. Her mother-in-law was already taking up permanent space in one of their bedrooms!*

If I had been this young lady, I would have seriously considered packing up the kids and leaving the house until all of the relatives had departed. But she stayed! She most surely had been brainwashed to welcome any and all without complaint and to bend over backward to make certain everyone was comfortable, housed, fed and content.

> *Alma was quite upset when her husband, Clayton, announced that an old friend of his from Chicago — someone he hadn't seen or heard from in twenty years, was coming to spend the night with them because this guy wanted to visit another friend in nearby Del Mar. "Why isn't he staying with his friend in Del Mar?" Alma asked. "Because he's my friend." was Clayton's reply. Alma then reminded him that their grandchildren were scheduled*

to stay with them that weekend. Clayton brushed this off with, "No problem. The kids can sleep on the floor." Clayton told Alma she could just make her great enchilada casserole for dinner and then make a nice breakfast for everyone the next morning.

Alma's friends enveloped her with ideas of just how she could dump her old "doormat" behavior. They suggested that she take her grandchildren to a motel for the weekend and have fun visiting local museums. She also considered taking the kids to her other daughter's ranch for the weekend and letting Clayton entertain his friend by himself. Alma was wringing her hands. She had spent forty – something years jumping through Clayton's hospitality hoops. She was extremely annoyed by this latest imposition, but reluctant to express her irritation for fear of making him angry. Alma's hospitality patterns are determined by her husband's forceful personality and, by golly, he expects her to follow through with his plans. Since she did not act on the advice offered, Alma's resentment may emerge in another way at another time and "poor Clayton" won't know what hit him.

Alma did, however, take the first step in her recovery by realizing that she is stuck in hospitality patterns of her own making. Perhaps next time she will resolve to take some action in her own behalf. She could tell Clayton after the visit never again to expect her to entertain his company without consulting her first. She could also let him know what her plans and subsequent reaction would be if it happens again.

Gwen is another one who was (notice the past tense) beset with clinical symptoms of ADS.

Her husband consistently and chronically brought home stray people, just as some bring home stray animals, without first consulting his wife. One time he brought home a busload of people who had been stranded in their broken down vehicle on the way to a commune. Gwen fed these strays for two weeks until the bus was repaired. The marriage eventually ended in divorce.

Other things may have precipitated the end of the marriage, but a partner intent upon whimsically harboring the homeless without first consulting his wife could certainly hasten the idea of divorce.

Perhaps the self-inviters, people beset with "foot in door disease," are the most difficult to handle. They can usually be categorized as wranglers, interlopers, or refugees. Residents in vacation - spot destination areas are particularly at risk from anybody and everybody who dreams of an expense-free laid-back getaway. Hosts who find themselves arm-wrestled by those seeking free vacations or temporary shelter may well be disheartened and dismayed in the aftermath of the experience.

We who are afflicted by Advanced Doormat Syndrome (Note: This syndrome isn't cited in the Diagnostic and Statistical Manual of Mental Disorders) are particularly prone to exploitation and need to be wary of those plotting to abuse our generosity and good will. The time to establish some rules and strategies for dealing with guests who may turn out to be heavenly, hellish, or clueless is long before the visitors step off the airplane or arrive at the door. This applies to long-lost friends, shirt-tail relatives, or a bundle of close family folk.

Chester and Jewel were on their way to a conference when they decided to call their friends, Dorothy and Wayne and wrangle a mini- vacation before the conference began. Dorothy and Wayne set aside other plans and dutifully picked the couple up at the airport then fed and entertained them for four days (two days longer than planned) before the freeloaders finally rented a car and took themselves to the conference.

Dorothy and Wayne are doormats. They were irked because the burden of entertaining people they hadn't planned to invite was on them. They entertained guests who invited themselves and then spent their own time and money that had been planned and budgeted elsewhere.

By the time our house guests depart, ADS suffers may be offended, irritated, and angry. The ensuing bitterness may eventually transform our social inclinations into an unpleasant shadow of inhospitality, as we cease inviting visitors to our home. But that would defeat our purpose.

Remember who we are. We are people who love and need other people. We just need to find a way to break uncomfortable old patterns and develop a satisfying medium that allows us to enjoy entertaining and to feel comfortable with our house guests and ourselves.

So . . . how do we change our actions and rid ourselves of the dreaded Doormat Syndrome? The initial step, which I have taken, is to admit I have the problem – "I am a doormat."

If you can easily recall several occasions when having house guests in your own home have been unpleasant experiences because "things just didn't go the way you thought they would," you are probably a victim of ADS. For example, if you are wondering how you let yourself agree to entertaining your husband's first wife's cousin and her second husband for TEN LONG days, you are probably a doormat. If cousin and second husband arrive with two pet iguanas who will need their "cool space," and you crank up the air conditioner after hastily clearing out your sewing room, you are very likely a doormat. And, ten days later, if cousin and second husband receive word his job has been eliminated, and they need to stay with you indefinitely while they look for work your in your "lovely area," you are, like me, a candidate for doormat of the year.

The first step is admission. The second step is recall. Review past house guest experiences, looking at similar patterns that led you to be unhappy with your role as host/hostess.

For example, some people have trouble saying "no" when their adult offspring call to ask if they can "come home for the summer." Although this may mean a return to the old days as "child" sleeps late, eats you out of house and home, and parties until all hours, many parents accept this as inevitable.

Other people can't seem to put time limits on their visitors' lengths of stay. Most of us are able to manage a three day hiatus in our daily schedules to entertain and enjoy guests. Longer stays tend to disrupt the household schedule, introduce chaos into the family agenda and end in fatigue for those responsible for planning and preparing meals and keeping the house in order. The tired old aphorism, "After three days fish and house guests smell" is about right.

Maybe you have been appalled at your brother-in-law's table manners (He eats like a savage!) Or with the way your former college roommate "took over" your personal computer without even asking.

Write down what you think caused you to be unhappy in your role as host.

Now is the time to look for solutions to your house guest dilemmas.

Much of this book addresses problems posed by house guests, and some even come with tidy solutions. A few of these problems admittedly were mine. Most of them were told to me by friends and acquaintances and perfect and not so perfect strangers. Some people related incidents that were easy to categorize and had an obvious solution: "Yes, she was a teenager, but she was my niece. I never thought about locking up the liquor cabinet." Conversely, the behavior of some guests can be so bizarre that it could never have been anticipated by a hostess. For example, when one hostess saw her guest's puppy hit by a car, she immediately took the dog to a veterinarian for attention. The owner of the dog, her sister, took one look at the $300 bill from the vet, and announced she wouldn't think of paying it, "I just got him at an animal shelter last week. I'm not that attached," she said, by way of explanation. This poor hostess was in shock, due more to her sister's callous disregard for the fate of the puppy than for the bill she had to pay.

Most stories carry lessons, but, as we know, lessons are hard to learn. Many people invite an old college roommate or boyfriend to visit – someone last seen some forty years ago. When telling me about these visitors, most hostesses expressed shock and, usually, dismay, at how their friend had "changed." Still, this is a house guest invitation that many of us will issue.

Perhaps some of the stories in this book will alert you to difficult or desperate house guest situations and will help you anticipate potential problems – and solutions to those problems. As strange as some of them may seem, let me assure you that all of these situations actually happened – at least, someone told me they happened!

Though we think of the United States as a great melting pot of blended cultures and languages, these stories reveal that differences in traditions surface when people from diverse backgrounds are thrown together. Behavior that I may think of as disruptive or ill-mannered may be considered thoughtful or considerate in some countries. However, when our "best laid plans" end up skewed and uncomfortable, we can and must learn from the fallout. Remember: we are the people who want to entertain guests. We want to invite family and friends to share our homes for a short time. It adds interest to our lives; we want to celebrate both the beginning and the end of these interludes.

None of us want to be held hostage or blindsided by either the host or the guest. This book presents the self-protective side of hospitality.

And that self-protective side begins with self-control when it comes to inviting people into our homes. We who are door-mats must recognize our problem often begins with our unintentional verbal invitations. "Y'all come." The following chapter will deal with the invitation – this is where we begin to take control – we become the Decider – the Chooser.

Darlene Dennis

-two-

Y'ALL COME!
(CREATING EFFECTIVE INVITATIONS)

. . .It is a custom more
honored in the breach
than in the observance.

William Shakespeare
Hamlet (I, iv)

While informally researching this book, it became apparent that most of us extend spur of the moment verbal invitations to our potential house guests. Instead of taking time to plan and to write an invitation, we often resort to the casual "Y'all Come," or "Be sure to stay with us if you ever come out to California – or Boston – or Des Moines." These haphazard invitations, tossed out when we are feeling sociable and particularly generous, are usually taken as a polite remark and quickly forgotten.

However, some folks misinterpret "sweet talk" for the real thing. Whether sincerely extended or not, a follow-up call from the recipient means he has taken your invitation at face value. Get ready for the house guests you "invited" but never expected to receive!

These spontaneous flippant invitations are probably the number one cause of host trauma.

By definition, an off the cuff invitation usually means you have failed to clear this visit with other members of your own family (a mistake discussed in Chapter 1.) Your vague invitations are apt to, lead to confusion, resulting in disappointment for both you and your guest.

> "Kathy and Marc invited Joyce and Paul to spend a week at their place in Charleston during the holidays. Since Joyce and Paul had never been to the south, they were looking forward to visiting historic sites. The "Y'all Come" invitation was verbal and confusing. Kathy and Marc envisioned including their friends in their social whirl while Joyce and Paul thought they would be entertained by planned sightseeing excursions with their hosts driving them around the area. This amounted to mutual astigmatism that resulted in confusion and disappointment for both couples.

This is the kind of situation you want to prevent. However, if you should find yourself in the midst of being forced to follow through with a commitment that your ego on a mania binge or your out of control big mouth has foisted upon you, there is still a chance to keep the visit within your own boundaries.

You must immediately follow through with a written invitation which will allow you to set terms (dates and times) for the impending visit. This will help you establish good communication with the guests before they arrive, so you both have a satisfying house guest visit.

Of course, your real goal is to avoid situations like this which have led you down the path to your present condition, Advanced Doormat Syndrome. But there is a cure.

First, it is essential for those of us suffering from ADS to elimi-nate these unintentional non-invitations from our vernacular.

Failure to heed this advice means you will continue to face the grim reality of unanticipated house guests. So, it's settled. No more spontaneous invitations. And now to the cure: Communication through the INTENTIONAL INVITATION!

In the future, each time you invite house guests, it will be an "intentional invitation," not a spur of the moment afterthought. "Intent" means you plan ahead what you are going to say. You can be specific.

Begin to plan the invitation by considering your own time and budget boundaries, then seize control of your own destiny. Take time to answer all of the questions and fill in the blanks, so you will feel comfortable with your plan before you extend the invitation.

- I am inviting (the name/s of those invited):

  _____

- for (the length of time):

  _____

- so we can (what you plan to do) _____
  _____ during the visit.

- They will sleep:

  _____

- They will need (clothes and sports equipment):

  _____

- They will use (transportation for traveling around town):

  _____

- We will be together during:

  _____

- They will leave:

_____

Think of the invitation as a dance of intentions. The host (you) initiates the dance by extending an intentional invitation, usually in person or by telephone. The guest, having a clear understanding of the invitation, accepts. The host leads – the guest follows. Modify the steps (the dates, time, and who is invited), and finalize the invitation that will serve everyone in this pleasantly anticipated event.

An invitation is an informal contract that establishes the variables and the possible limits therein for the visitor.

As the host, you need to follow up the verbal invitation with a written invitation, either by e-mail, Fax, or letter. It reveals who in invited, when they are expected to arrive, and how long they are welcome to stay.

Your communication also includes some of the entertainment activities they might expect, along with transportation, food, and clothing issues. These written intentions (taken from the "fill in the blanks" you completed before you made the <u>intentional</u> verbal invitation) set the guidelines for the visit and should go far in reducing unforeseen glitches during the stay.

Have a calendar at hand to check dates. (You might ask your guests to forward a copy of their itinerary after they make their reservations after they have accepted your invitation.) When the written invitation is the initial contact, be sure to give the guest enough time to plan head to make the visit.

The operative "magic word" in the invitation as well as throughout the visit is "Let"...

. . . as in – "We will 'let' you rent a car at the airport," or, "There wasn't time to prepare for your visit, so I'll 'let' you make up your bed while I gather together a snack."

"Let" is a word that comes in handy in a variety of ways and with folks of all ages. If, however, the host is confronted with a guest who is planning to "let" him pay for all and do it all, there needs to be a polite but firm response. Return this sort of presumptuous attitude with, "That won't be possible, we will have to 'let' you take care of that."

If this is a reciprocal visit, the host now takes a turn at extending hospitality as close as possible to that which he has formerly enjoyed.

When extending the follow-up written invitation, all details should be included.

The following invitation covers most of the concerns of a visit, i.e. food, entertainment, wardrobe and transportation.

> *Hi Phyllis and Eric:*
>
> *It was good talking with you Thursday evening. At last you are going to visit us! It will be fun to catch up on family news with my little sister and laugh at Eric's new collection of bad jokes. Eric, I remember you are allergic to milk products, so we will try to plan menus accordingly. While you are here, we will attend a production at our local theater, visit a museum or two at our beautiful park and probably have dinner one night at the local Indian Casino. It is often chilly here in the evening (even in summer), so plan to bring a light jacket, swimwear for the beach, sports wear for touring around town and one*

dressy outfit for dinner out and the theater. Because we won't be able to join you when you visit the tourist sites and we will be using both of our cars, we will let you pick up a rental car at the airport and drive out to our home in time for drinks before dinner on the 8th. We will say good-bye after brunch on Sunday the 15th. Remember to bring pictures of the kids.

Love,

Sis

When an invitation is extended, it needs to include the stated objective or centerpiece of the visit.

Dear Jane:

Could you set aside the weekend of the 6th of next month from Friday evening until Sunday noon to come help me sort through the inherited antiques and bric-a-brac in the shed out behind my house? I know you have just the eye to tell me what should go to the antique dealer, what to give to the thrift shop and what to toss out. I'm hoping that you find a few collectables for your own home as a reward for your expertise.

I also want to treat you to a new play at our own little theater. I'll fix some of my favorite dishes for you and we can catch up on the latest news. Bring jeans for work and a dress for the theater. I know you don't eat anchovies, so I'll leave those out of my Caesar salad.

If this date doesn't work for you, we can try for another weekend soon.

It will be so nice to be with you again.

Betty

Betty's objective is to have her friend help her clean out the shed. She makes it enticing and further offers to repay her kindness with a ticket to the theater.

Then there is the casual get-together where everyone pitches in to create a memorable visit.

Hi Joe:

The big game is on the 10th of next month and I am hoping you will be free to come on out and stay for the weekend. Bob, Doug, and Ken are planning to be here. You can plan on a weekend of partying. When we don't eat out we'll take turns cooking, so bring your great chili recipe.

I can pick you up and deliver you to the airport.

Get back to me ASAP so I can reserve tickets in your name.

Ben

Ben's motives for inviting his buddies for the weekend are clear. He wants his friends to join him for the game and do some partying. The guys will surely know what clothes are appropriate and they will all chip in on some of the food and cooking. He has also covered the issue of transportation.

Remember to be very clear about beginning and ending dates and times as well as exactly who is invited.

If couples who have children are being invited sans the kids, be sure and say so — delicately. Excluding children and animals from the guest list may require exceptional diplomatic skill. Feelings are often fragile when it comes to ruling out little ones or canine and feline family members for a house guest visit. It is always prudent to anticipate problems in advance. This may be necessary if guests are bringing pets or children.

Explicitly state the conditions for the visit.

Example: (No pets; No pit bulls, snakes, iguanas, or llamas!)

Hazards: (since our pool area is not fenced, we cannot entertain children who are not excellent swimmers.) Guests also need to know if the host has animals since some folks are allergic to animal dander which can raise havoc and make them miserable.

The following suggestions for stepping lightly around these issues may prove helpful.

> *"We are looking forward to a weekend of adult conversation and entertainment. We hope that you will be able to find someone to take care of the children while you visit us. If not, we will try to catch you at a later date."*

Or,

> *"We know that Fi Fi is considered a member of your family and we will make arrangements for a sleeping place for her. You, of course, will be in charge of the food, water, and walks. The kids will just love your sweet English Sheep Dog."*

Or,

> *"We know that you often travel with Fi Fi, but our home simply isn't set up to entertain guests with animals. We hope that you will be able to find other accommodations for your darling dog while you visit us. There is a wonderful kennel nearby and we can supply the number so you can make reservations for Fi Fi for the duration of your visit if she has to accompany you."*

Or,

> *"Our condominium complex forbids pets, so it will be impossible to include Puff or Fi Fi in this invitation."*

Or,

> *"Since we are situated on a golf course which is the playground for hungry coyotes from dusk 'till dawn, you will probably prefer not to bring your dog."*

Or,

> *"We do want to alert you to the fact that a dog (name the breed) and two cats are members of our family. They enjoy playing with children, so we are looking forward to your entire family mingling with ours."*

Or,

> *"Our cocker spaniel is snappish with children. While we will attempt to keep him in separate quarters, this is his home and we want you to make your own decisions about whether or not to join us under these circumstances."*

One young woman who was entertaining a suitor for a weekend discovered that he was allergic to her precious cats. The two cats had to stay outside for the duration of his visit. Her suitor also indicated that he would have a difficult time if they visited a friend of hers who had dogs. She told this young man that she had too many rough edges for him and the relationship was terminated.

Occasionally there are guests who smoke and hosts who find smoke in their homes beyond offensive.

This is an issue that needs to be clearly addressed in the invitation.

Dear Marilyn:

We will meet your plane at 11:00 P.M. on Sunday. You will be exhausted from such a long flight, so plans for Monday are designed to be relaxing. I've made an appointment for you to have a manicure and pedicure if that is to your liking. After that we can do a little shopping and have a light lunch before heading up the mountain to visit Joe and the kids. Later we can meander over to the casino for a bit of gambling and dinner. For the rest of the week we will be having dinner with our friends, attending a wonderful new production of the musical, Carmen, spending one day at the art museum and allowing some time for the beach. We will deliver you back at the airport on Saturday morning. By the way, we know that you are a smoker. Since we don't allow smoking in the house, we will let you take your ashtray out to the deck and enjoy your cigarettes there.

Hugs,

Stephanie

It is possible to have house guests that want to use your home primarily as a B&B. Sadly, these folks won't be paying for their bed. I am referring primarily to close friends or your own children who may be visiting your area while they attend a conference, a wedding, etc. On these occasions you don't have to spend time or money entertaining, but you have elected to help them save money by allowing them to use your guest room as a hotel or a hostel (without room service, of course.) Be certain to make it clear in your written invitation they will be strictly on their own when it comes to food, transportation, and entertainment

Dear Pricilla and Peter:

It's good to know that you will be in our area for a few days. We won't be able to entertain you as "real" guests because of our own intense schedule. If you would like to save the price of a hotel, however, you are welcome to use our guest room from the 5th to the 8th. You will need to rent a car at the airport since we have a family policy of not lending ours. This will definitely be a "No Frills" visit. We will leave the back light on. The backdoor will be open. (We don't issue house keys either). Your room is to the left at the top of the stairs. There are several nice ethnic restaurants close by.

We are light sleepers and we both have heavy work schedules, so, if you come in after we have gone to bed, please close the door quietly and tread lightly up the stairs.

Let us know by next Thursday if you plan to stay here.

Our Best,
Luke and Lucy

On occasion a family emergency may occur, and it might be necessary to renege on the invitation.

When this happens, inform your invited guests immediately so they can make other plans.

We are so sorry to have to cancel our invitation for you to stay with us next week. John has been hospitalized with a heart ailment and the doctors are predicting a slow recovery. The household is in turmoil; I'm simply not up to entertaining. I hope we will be able to reschedule your vacation here in the future.

Or,

*The weather has turned frightful and the forecasters
predict this torrential rain will continue for the next two
weeks. Due to flooding, visiting the wonderful tourist
sites in the area is impossible so we suggest you reschedule
your visit when our sunshine returns.*

*Another possible reason for a host to back-pedal on an invitation
is if, at the last minute, the guests have unexpected or unrealistic
expectations for the visit and/or accommodations.*

*Lois, who spends little time at home, was expecting
visitors for a two week stay. At the last moment, they
called to "let" her know they are both vegetarians. She
was beside herself with irritation. It would have been
entirely acceptable if she had told them that it would
be impossible for her to accommodate their dietary
needs. She then could have rescinded the invitations by
suggesting nearby hotel accommodations.*

One memorable experience happened long ago. I dialed a
wrong number. A man picked up the phone and instead of the
usual, "Hello" or "The Smith residence," He said, "The Smiths
aren't at home. The Smiths can't pick you up at the airport. The
Smith's aren't entertaining." I laughed and told him, probably
much to his relief, that I had dialed the wrong number. He went
on to explain that the Smith's had had an onslaught of company
and they were tired of eating chicken (probably an inexpensive
meal for company); they just wanted to finish playing a family
game of Parcheesi.

The written invitation is designed to keep everyone in step.
There should be no need for last minute choreography around
such matters as the length of the visit, who is or is not invited,

food fetishes, wardrobe needs, entertainment options, or that vague killer: expectations.

Most of us who have been held hostage may require a bit of time along with practice to transform ourselves into the person who rules her own turf. During that transition period, we may find ourselves backsliding and the victim of yet another "y'all come." Or, we may be caught off guard and accept a refugee or interloper into our midst. It takes only one or two uncomfortable experiences for interest in entertaining house guests to dwindle. There are some who eschew entertaining house guests altogether. They have their own reasons and methods for not playing the role of host or hostess.

Once we have opened the doors to our chosen guests and are experiencing the pleasure and honor of their company, grousing is not allowed, protesting is not allowed, and letting down is not allowed. Even though we may encounter unexpected or even shocking behavior that is out of line with our own standards, the requirement for the host is a stiff upper lip and an underlying sense of humor – unless, of course, the behavior is malicious, unethical or dangerous. And, just think: it's possible to turn all that hidden rage into a funny story you can regale friends with at another time. As the host, you must be hospitable to your guests.

DODGING THE ROLE OF HOSPITALITY HOST/ESS

There are some, who may, from time to time, enjoy entertaining small groups for luncheons, brunches, cocktail parties or dinners, but avoid entertaining house guests. Some people have a large family or many friends, but they cleverly manage to avoid overnight or longer commitments. Are they bad people? Certainly not; many of them hug their privacy and simply prefer to avoid tripping over guests. While they may care about seeing friends for a few hours, they do not want to share their territory for longer than it takes to serve cocktails or a brief meal. Some hospitality dodgers may have creative approaches to closing their home to outsiders or family insiders.

Annie, a professional cook in Granby, Massachusetts entertains large numbers of her extended family during all of the holidays. Her profession and her hobby coalesce for great get-togethers at her bountiful table. Annie extended her dining room by knocking out the wall to her spare room and linking it to the hallway and the existing dining room. She cleverly created a space that would accommodate a large table and simultaneously do away with the guest room. In spite of the fact that she is an open handed, generous hearted sharer and entertainer, her attitude toward house guests is something else.

Annie's view is, "As soon as you own your own home and have an extra room, every vagabond knocks on the door looking for a place to stay." Annie frequently entertains her friends and family, employing her culinary expertise, but no one stays overnight.

Linda has been divorced and living alone for twenty-five years. She owns a one bedroom condominium that precludes inviting even her children to stay as house guests. She loves her kids, but when they come to town, they have to stay in a hotel.

Roxanne is another one who feels she has insulated herself from entertaining house guests. She just rented out half of her home, leaving herself living space –with one bedroom. She feels that only those who are college age or younger would suggest using her living room for temporary sleeping quarters using sleeping bags. She feels she has secured her privacy and protected herself from those who might attempt to wrangle, interlope or establish a role as refugees. He grown children stay in a hotel when they visit.

Many years ago when my husband was stationed in Beeville, Texas, I recall that a local couple built a beautiful new custom home — with only one bedroom. It was the talk of both the local and navy communities. Whoever in this day and age heard of a beautiful house with only one bedroom? How could people who live in a house like that and entertain house guests? Sleeping bags on the living room floor aside, they can't. These clever non-hosts probably had a method in their creative madness. They were, more than likely, hospitality dodgers who had their fill of houseguests and were determined to retain their privacy.

Others have turned rooms that would ordinarily serve as guest rooms into offices with wall to wall desk and bookshelves, a game room complete with pool table, a sewing room with stacks of materials, or a workout room full of treadmills, rowing machines, and weight-lifting equipment.

Judy has an entirely different tactic for excluding house guests. She never extends an invitation, but if anyone calls to wrangle a stay at her place, she simply says, "You're welcome to stay with us, but I need to tell you that our cat sleeps in the extra bedroom. She sheds terribly and so there is usually cat hair everywhere. She is our pet and has the run of the house. Also, you are apt to have her pounce into bed with you in the middle of the night." For years now, Judy hasn't had anyone other than her cat sleeping in that room

In spite of the warm hospitality that southerners are expected to exude from every pore, Stella in Tennessee was a bona fide rebel.

It wasn't just Damn Yankees, but everyone who came to her door encountered the unwelcome mat that read, "GO AWAY!" She left a note for those who delivered boxes to just leave them on her doorstep. Stella had no ambition to play the role of southern "Miss Hospitality." She didn't want company and definitely not house guests. She considered guests a troublesome nuisance.

This attitude was an embarrassment to her daughter, but Stella didn't care. Every one of us has unique personal and social requirements. Within our own homes, we are privileged to determine if we want to entertain guests.

Hospitality dodgers may be generous and have fine social skills, but for their own reasons may simply prefer not to have others spend any length of time in their space. Hopefully we are all capable of appreciating and respecting their privacy

Every so often, friends or family may select your home as a vacation spot without you first having the bright idea to invite them. While some of these unintended visits may be welcome, others might be considered inconvenient and intrusive. What do you do when family, friends, and even acquaintances decide to "honor" you with an unexpected or unwelcome visit? The problems of dealing with those wranglers, interlopers, freeloaders and refugees determined to impose on the "doormats" of the world are set down in the next few chapters.

-three-

WILY WRANGLERS AND
SELF INVITERS

And when I found the door was locked,
I pulled and pushed and kicked and knocked.
And when I found the door was shut,
I tried to turn the handle, but...

Lewis Carrol,
Through the Looking Glass Part II

When you live in an area with year round sunshine, there could always be a surge of visitors eager to enjoy your hospitality.

If it is holiday time and the allure of your area is skiing, hunting, racing, or a beautiful beach, there may be a flood of requests from eager free-loaders seeking the gratis guest quarters while they indulge in a favorite hobby or sport.

So what are the strategies for dealing with these wily invitation wranglers — those cunning self-inviters? They often employ a sneak attack when calling with the definite idea that your home would be the perfect place for a cut-rate vacation. A private home is usually less expensive than Motel 6.

Before you have an opportunity to say "yes" to another bad bargain, learn to say "no" to opportunists who expect hospitality that hasn't been volunteered.

Interlopers just show up and refugees are temporarily homeless, but the self-inviters call ahead with their intentions. These wranglers may be family, close friends, so-so acquaintances, or friends of friends. The target host learns that he is expected to rearrange his schedule and provide all of the amenities for a houseguest even though the visit was not his idea.

Will he allow himself to be held hostage in his own home, providing sleeping space, food and entertainment for those he would rather avoid? Will he curl his mouth in an insincere smile, step back and welcome the unwelcome or will he stick up for his territorial rights and excuse himself from having his terrain invaded and his pocket picked?

Self-inviting is a presumptuous and, more often than not, an offensive attempt to access entertainment and free sleeping space.

> *A nephew called to ask Ross, an elderly widower, if he and his wife could visit him in Del Mar. Ross hadn't seen this man, now fifty, in more than thirty years and didn't feel like entertaining the couple in his home, so he arranged to have them stay at the nearby hotel at his expense. He also provided them with tickets for the San Diego Zoo, a courtesy lost on this couple who barely uttered "thanks."*

Ross' relatives had called and self-invited and put him on the spot. Friends and relatives listening to this tale of aggravation told Ross that the next time this happens he needs to just say, "No." But Ross is old school and demurs from anything that might appear ungracious or niggardly. This is a personal note to the Ross's of the world: It's okay to say, "Sure, I would enjoy seeing you. Where are you staying? Call when you get settled, and maybe we can touch base for brunch or dinner" You are under no obligation to entertain them in your home, pay for their hotel accommodations, or underwrite their vacation.

Those who presume that the household of a family member or friend is always open to them should be apprised of their transgressions.

If you are blindsided by a wrangling self-inviter, be prepared for the offender to be offended if you resist his distasteful attempt to intrude into your private space. Rejecting and being rejected usually ranges from uncomfortable to miserable for everyone involved. However, you can learn to set and maintain boundaries without feeling guilty.

Julie, who lives in Tampa, Florida received a call from her cousin, Martha, in Minnesota, announcing that she was planning a February visit to Tampa to escape the blustery winter. Julie is in her seventies; her husband is in his eighties. Julie decided she really didn't want company. She suggested to Martha that a visit would be difficult at this time. Martha huffed, "Do you mean that your house isn't open to family like me?" They hung up with the understanding that Martha would be there for a visit at the end of February.

Julie took a deep breath. After she and her husband briefly discussed the dilemma, she e-mailed this message to Martha: "We think you had better scrub your planned trip. Neither of us looks forward to entertaining house guests. We prefer our live alone lifestyle; overnight guests are all we are prepared to entertain. At our age, we are becoming less social."

Martha could have pursued another strategy. She could have made arrangements to stay in a hotel in Tampa for a week in February and then called Julie to let her know that she would like to invite her and her husband for dinner one night while she was there. Julie then might have taken the opportunity to invite her cousin to stay at their home for a couple of days. By trying to wrangle an invitation, Martha set herself up to be wounded.

Slipping into near depression when faced with the onslaught of houseguests isn't worth saving face when defensive excuses aren't on the tip of the tongue.

Aggressive wranglers are apt to initiate their intentions by calling and asking leading questions that will put the intended host in a position to comply with their plans. The following are some possible examples:

1. Will you be home during July? We are thinking of coming out.

2. What are your plans for the holidays? We thought it might be fun to get together.

3. We know you have a guest house and are wondering if we could stay there during Lenny's vacation in June.

4. We haven't seen you in such a long time; we are thinking of spending our vacation with you.

5. Our daughter is planning on attending the university that is close to you. We are wondering if we could stay with you while we get her situated in her dorm.

6. The skiing should be great in January. We would like to visit you at your cabin and enjoy a few runs down the slopes.

7. Our kids are out of school for a week in April and the two of them would like to stay with you in Naples for Spring break.

8. We are going to be in Seattle on July 10th and 12th. We are hoping that the Smith Inn is available to us.

Picking up the phone and hearing someone at the other end attempting to wrangle an invitation is apt to send many of us into a dither. This loss of composure is a big factor in prompting us to yammer, "Y'all Come" or "Sure, come on out, We'd love to see you," when what you really relish is your own routine or solitude.

What is a less than enthusiastic target host to do when confronted by a brash, bold request to use his residence as a cheap vacation spot?

1. Scouts, you must BE PREPARED!.

2. Screen your calls. (Many people use a message machine) or avoid answering the telephone when it rings.

3. You might be better pleased with yourself if you can manage to begin the refusal with something soft and sweet such as, "Gee, we would love to have you here , but" . . . then think of a reason not to entertain the self-inviters in your home. Better yet, keep a written list of plausible excuses by the phone and use it!

Mary Ruth and Neil have a summer home on a lake in northern Wisconsin. Over the years they have learned to establish their own boundaries while still enjoying family and friends in the area. Mary Ruth extends the invitations telling each person to bring their specialty dish if it's a weekend visit. She also lets her guests know that they are to bring their own beverages, linens and extra beach towels. Guests are welcome to use the speed boat, but they must have it filled with gas. When uninvited folks appear at the door, Mary Ruth has learned to say that they are expecting a house full and there is no where for them to sleep. She then tells them they must call next time before coming. She says this gives her time to think whether she wants to entertain them and, if not, she has an easier opportunity to politely decline their self-invitation.

Unless boundaries are firmly established, these self-inviters are apt to make your residence their summer or winter retreat, depending on which destination area you are blessed with. If this is fun for you, fine. If not, think through the situation and decide on a new strategy.

Doug and Sue Martin hadn't seen Sharon and Al Boggs for twenty years. Sharon called to say that their son was entering a university in the same city where Doug and Sue lived and she asked if they could came and stay with them. The initial phone call failed to set any dates or time frame. One day – out of the blue – Sharon called saying they would arrive the next day and would be staying for ten days. Sue told the Boggs' that they hadn't expected them at that time, so while they were welcome to stay at the house. Doug and Sue had other plans and were not providing meals or any entertainment.

The Boggs' were extremely forward in assuming that the Martins would be willing to open their home to them after not seeing them for twenty years. They were extremely rude in not setting down the dates earlier so the Martins could make advance preparation or excuses. The wrangling Boggs' represents a prime example of a couple with a callous disregard for the host. They view their target as a person who is expected to provide the guest with gratis accommodations so they can conduct their business in the area without much cost.

While Sue Martin deftly handled the situation, she probably dropped the ball when the first call came from the Boggs. If she had asked exactly when the Boggs planned to be in the city and for how long, she would have created an opportunity to refuse the visit or to issue a follow-up invitation establishing the parameters for the visit.

Every situation is different as may be seen in the following example:

> *Ellie has a large home on a beautiful beach that over-looks a famous racetrack. She told me that just before racing season she is deluged with calls from "friends" that she hasn't heard from all year. The racing season is approaching and they want to visit her. She has a defi-nite response which is: "I don't entertain guests during the racing season." Ellie's former husband is a horse trainer and many of these self-inviters who are aware of this connection are intent upon being entertained in her home as well as the Turf Club. This attitude is beyond presumptuous because entertaining anyone in this manner is extremely expensive even if you are a member of the Turf Club. Since many of these "self-inviters" are well to do, Ellie's theory is that the wealthiest people also have a built-in sense of entitlement. They expect folks to bend over backward and provide everything for free.*

Often we, as hosts, are expected to roll out the welcome mat for those who are chronically pushy and presumptuous. These people assume that free hospitality is available any time they decide to visit. They need to be dealt with firmly.

One guest who invited herself to visit the Galsters and then stayed for ten days told everyone she met during her stay that she was returning in December. The Galsters hadn't invited her for the initial stay, nor for a second in December.

The hostess was prepared. The guest stood at the door on her way out and failed to say "Thank you." The awkward empty air space was covered by Mrs. Galster saying, "Have a nice trip home." The guest then promptly staged her come-back plan, "Oh, I'll be back in December."

The hostess responded with, "When in December?"

This overbearing self-inviter replied, "Well, maybe early December. Why?

Mrs. Galster's reply was, "Because we won't be here for Christmas."

Madam Arrogant then wanted to know where they were going. The hostess simply told her, "I don't know, but I'm not doing Christmas."

With that, the offended wrangler clamped her jaw shut, turned on her heel and left — without so much as a word of gratitude for the ten day twenty-four/seven bend over backward hospitality.

A couple of years later this person did graciously host the Galsters for three days in her lovely home. Before they left, however, she wanted to know if she and her significant other could visit them for a week over Christmas. The Galsters were stuck. The guests arrived, they were entertained, the hosts endured, and they're done.

On occasion there is a reverse attitude.

Joanie's friend from Minnesota called to say that she and a chum were coming to Del Mar for a week. They already had reservations at a nearby hotel, but wondered if they would have a chance to see Joanie and her husband while they were in the area. Joanie was upset that they weren't planning to stay with her and implored them to give up the hotel and take advantage of her two guest rooms. She also made arrangements to chauffeur these guests around town during the visit.

There are times when putting out feelers for a place to stay may be just fine and may work well for both guest and host. Lynn was in a muddle and in search of a bed so she could attend a conference. She put out the word via e-mail and the response was the houseguest visit she had hoped for. This is her experience:

Last week I spent a few days in Santa Barbara, taking a wonderful course. I couldn't really afford both tuition and hotel costs, so I sent out an e-mail to my classmates, asking for a cheap bed. I got one! Stacey wrote and said she had a spare room I could stay in. When I got there, she showed me her spare room, cum office, cum storage room, cum closet. It was comfortable and I slept well the whole week. I wish every woman I know could give herself permission to be a minimalist host.

This story differs from the other "wrangler" anecdotes because Stacey actually invited Lynn to stay after she issued a general request.

Stephanie is married to a prominent physician and is required to entertain houseguests so often than that she has dubbed their home "The Thompson Manor." She e-mailed me the following:

"A friend and his wife have spent at least thirteen days at Thompson Manor during the last year and have never bought us a meal or brought a hostess gift. I did ask them to change the sheets at the end of their last visit as we had back to back guests."

What follows is a recent exchange of e-mails Stephanie sent me.

Hi Stephanie:

I hope you had a great time in France. It sounds like you will be having a busy summer. There is a three day workshop near your house that we are planning to attend. It is August 3-5, which I believe is Friday to Sunday. It is one of those long conferences — 9 am to 11 pm each day. Will you be around? Can we stay at your house? If you are around and not too busy, we can visit before and/or after the workshop. Maybe if we get there early enough on Thursday, I can do some research for you.

Mark

Stephanie replied:

Hi Mark:

I spoke to my nephew and his fiancé just before I got your e-mail. This is the couple who were here right after your last visit. I offered to let them stay the first few weeks of August – until they find an apartment. I wish I could have offered to have you stay. The Motel 6 is right by Enid and David Streets and has the lowest rate I've seen in town – if that is of any help.

*What is the seminar about? Should you have time
for dinner or lunch during that weekend, let us know and
we will meet you somewhere.*

Three cheers for Stephanie. She refused to be taken to the
cleaners again by these freeloading wranglers. Notice that she
graciously told them how sorry she was that she was unable to
comply with their wishes and expectations.

My face still glows red when I confess I was a self inviter
during the late 50's. I was engaged to a naval aviator stationed
on St. Simons Island, Georgia and in those days a girl was a
virgin until she marched down the aisle in a white gown. Staying
with a boyfriend in a motel was unheard of. I unabashedly
invited myself (several times) to visit Gloria and Art Keown in
order to be with my fiancé. They were gracious, generous and
hospitable and I don't remember if I ever even wrote them a
thank you note or brought a hostess gift.

Possible responses for inveterate wranglers:

1. Our time for entertaining family and friends as
houseguests has passed.

2. We have a full season planned and there is no
time for company. If you do come to our region
and stay at the local motel, give us a call; perhaps
we could meet for lunch or brunch one day.

3. We are done in; if you want to come to town, stay
at a hotel and invite us for the holiday dinner at a
swanky restaurant, we would gladly accept your
invitation. Otherwise, we are hanging out a home
– alone and relishing our solitude.

4. Avoid saying that you don't have guest accommodations. Some intrepid wranglers will have their
   sleeping bags ready to toss on the living room
   floor.

No matter the destination, the self-inviter represents an offensive intrusion in the plans of the host family.

If these overstepping offenders are insulted by those who maintain their own household boundaries by refusing to entertain uninvited house guests, then so be it. It's never too late to learn that that the aim of accessing accommodations without invitation is basically rude and potential victims are not prepared or thrilled about willy-nilly underwriting someone else's vacation.

The Smiths said they would love to have us . . .

-four-

INTERLOPERS AND FREELOADERS

I thank you for your company;
 but good faith,
I had as lief have been myself alone.

William Shakespeare
As You Like It
(III, ii)

When wrangling failed to provide Jeremy and Jennifer Jones with an invitation to stay with their friends, the Bowers, they switched to the interloper mode. They're darn lucky they didn't wind up in jail.

Jeremy and Jennifer, called their friends, the Bowers, who lived in Boston to let them know their plans to attend a psychiatric convention in their area. Sally Bower told them that they would love to have them stay at their place, but that they would be out of town during the time the convention was scheduled. Sally and Lou left town for two weeks; when they returned home, a neighbor told them that they had noticed strange people staying at their house while they were away.

The neighbor asked these people who they were and learned that Jeffery and Jennifer had let themselves into the Bower house through an unlocked window. They stayed in the Bower's home for the duration of the psychiatric convention. Sally said that though she didn't mind, she thought their behavior was odd. Also, the Jones' failed to tell them what they had done and never bothered to write a thank you note.

Drop-in is the euphemistic term for those interlopers and free-loaders who show up at the door without an invitation!

Whether it is for an afternoon drink, dinner, or an extended stay, the clear intent of hospitality violators is to hold the host hostage for a period of time. These unconscionable uninvited are the bona fide insurgents on the category menu of houseg-uests. Oddly, a few of these people cling to the view that "The folks will be so glad to see me," or "I'm no trouble and there is always room for one more."

If you are baffled by scroungers who have appeared unex-pectedly at your home, it's fine to ask, "How is it you decided to come for a visit without advance notice?" Even when we are caught off guard, posing such a question seems like bad manners to most of us who have been programmed to "always be polite." Not to worry, this is the time to be a notch less than, enthusi-astic about a drop in. If you have been selected as a prospec-tive host/victim, you are certainly entitled to an explanation of the underpinnings of the visitors' logic. If you don't want to act as host and entertain these folks, it is within your inalien-able boundary rights to say so —even at the risk of offending the potential interlopers. No explanation is really needed for refusing to entertain these intractable insurgents except, "We are not prepared to entertain you."

Interlopers and freeloaders disrupt the personal social scene.

They frequently employ charm and creative excuses to weasel their way into a home where they slowly but surely become a weapon of mass family destruction. Their prolonged presence quickly decimates the household budget and the family's peace of mind. These folks breathe the hosts' oxygen, eat their food, crowd their space and usurp their privacy while somehow imagining that the host family feels privileged to entertain them in style. They are shameless marauders, consistently manifesting unconscionable behaviors.

These miserly moochers operate by the old Arab adage of "A host is responsible for the food, shelter and safety of his guests as long as they are in his tent — even if the guests are his enemy." This maxim is probably embedded in their DNA. Their attitude is "you owe me," or "you are so fortunate to have the honor of feeding, housing and entertaining me."

The interloper/freeloader is first and foremost a charming predator.

We take many a risk when we allow the interloper (sometimes known as *couch surfer)* entry into our home. The critical question is, why let these uninvited in the door?

After spending a long week teaching 3^(rd) graders, Sharon was changing clothes and planning a light dinner for herself when the doorbell rang. She found, Josephine, a former colleague, standing at her door, her suitcase in hand; "My son is in the hospital here and I knew you would put me up for the weekend so I can visit him." Josephine announced. It turned out that she had been staying with another friend who had dropped her off on Sharon's doorstep. Flustered, Sharon let her in the door, told the intruder that she was just fixing a sandwich for dinner and asked if she would like to join her. Josephine immediately said, "Why don't we go over to the casino and have dinner?" While this might have been a clear red flag, Sharon was an innocent, so she agreed. Bingo! Sharon ended up paying for dinner and "lending" Josephine gambling money. After three weeks of loaning Josephine money and acting as her chauffeur, Sharon announced her intention to leave town on a short vacation. She told Josephine that she would have to move on. Unperturbed, Josephine asked if she could just stay at Sharon's while she was away. Fed up with catering to a "scrounger," Sharon refused the request, then drove Josephine to the house of another "friend," and dropped her off.

Occasionally Josephine, the freeloader, still calls Sharon asking to borrow money. Having learned her lesson, Sharon refuses. While this might seem like a worst case scenario, interloper transgressions are legendary.

One would think that when perfect strangers invade a home, the residents would rebel. But this doesn't always happen right away:

Upon returning home from a theater outing, Margaret and Tom Murphy saw through the window — instead of the babysitter — two strangers sitting in their living room. Most rational people would have immediately called the SWAT team, but not Margaret and Tom. When they questioned these two intruders in their living room, it turned out they were Sam and Kasha from Sweden. They had met a friend of Margaret's on the East coast who suggested they stop to visit the Murphy's when they got to California. This chutzpah had served them well from Europe to America and then from the East coast to the West coast! In their travels around the world on a shoestring, they had no problem inviting themselves into the homes of total strangers! Sounds ridiculous? A newspaper back east had even printed a laudatory feature article on this couple, their travels and their methods of seeking out places to stay. When they arrived at Margaret and Tom's they simply dismissed the babysitter and waited for their "elected" hosts to return. They stayed with the Murphy's for two weeks. At one point, Sam happened to mention that it was his birthday, so Tom and Margaret treated this couple to a day at Disneyland. Finally, Margaret told the couple they, would have to leave because the Murphy's were leaving town. No problem, the couple simply moved on up the coast to Malibu for a stay with a star of a television series whose wife was from Sweden. Kasha knew one of the wife's relatives and used it as a bridge for entry. Even though Sam and Kasha were very accommodating house guests, helping with the dishes, and other household chores, they were definitely accomplished interloper/free loaders!

THE DANGERS OF LIVING IN A DESTINATION LOCATION

It is a truth universally held by freeloaders that a family in a geographically attractive area in possession of an extra sleeping space must be in want of houseguests. Never mind that the family may prefer privacy. That extra bedroom or guest room or guest house is considered the rightful property of some of these indefatigable parasites. Just as wily predators in the animal kingdom use their cunning to lure their prey; these uninvited marauders are alert and usually bereft of anything resembling a normal social conscience as they move for the kill. They will wriggle a foot in your door, push their way into your sanctuary and manage to set up residence that may range from temporary to permanent. It somehow fails to register with these insensitive dolts that their presence is not wanted, and after several days (the classical three), they are no longer welcome.

Connie and Don Norton moved from Michigan to a lovely home in Denver which had a whole basement apartment. Within a year, the Norton's found they were entertaining a stream of in 'n out houseguests. One second cousin from Michigan arrived with his wife and stayed a week. They then drove off to visit his brother in Colorado Springs. Oops, the brother and his family were out of town, so they returned to the Norton accommodations for another week. Then off they went to Colorado Springs and a "no response knock" at the brother's door. Back they went to Denver. Connie and Don "entertained" this second cousin and his wife for a full month. The last time they left, Connie went to the beauty parlor. On her way out the door, she told Don to call her if they returned because she was going to check into a motel. She was determined not to cook another meal for these freeloaders.

THE YEARLY PLAGUE OF LOCUSTS WITH SHELLS

Freeloaders wear many masks, and have representatives from every level of society; they employ a variety of tactics and flimsy excuses for their hospitality trespassing.

Bonnie, in Denver, is plagued by an interloper/freeloader with a trailer. This particular marauder happens to be her brother who appears in the early summer, parks his rig in her backyard, hooks up to her electricity and

remains for the season – using her kitchen and bath-
room. But because the free loader is her brother, Bonnie
feels guilty about feeling uneasy with the state of affairs
and tolerates the uncomfortable situation of having her
territory, time, privacy and provisions invaded.

Bonnie needs to strengthen her resolve and, at the very least, tell her brother that if he is going to stay for the summer, that she will charge him for half the water and electric bills. She could also tell him that she would be more comfortable if he parked his rig at a trailer park for the summer. They would then be able to visit back and forth; Bonnie would retain her privacy and eliminate being stuck for extra utility bills.

Ben has a distant relative, Jennifer. She frequently arrives at Ben and Sue's home in a camper from the opposite coast with her current significant other in tow.

On one occasion, they immediately took over the
premises using the phone to conduct their business, using
the laundry facilities, raiding the refrigerator and with
no notice, appearing for meals if it suited them. Finally,
after two weeks, Sue went a bit berserk when Jennifer
started stuffing things in the washer. Sue screamed,
"Don't use my washer!" Of course, it wasn't the issue
of using the washing machine, but using the laundry
facilities without permission had become a symbol of the
invasive nature of the "freeloader's" ongoing behaviors.
Ben took care of the problem by finally telling these two,
"The laundry is closed; the kitchen is closed; the hotel is
closed; the trailer park will welcome you."

Apparently others with trailers and a yen to travel on the cheap are adept at interloping and freeloading.

It was the dinner hour when a car with a trailer attached rolled up into the yard of Janet and Gill Darwin who live in North Mississippi. A woman stepped out and said that mutual friends of theirs suggested that she stop there. She asked if she could hook up her trailer to their facilities for a few days while she toured the area. The Darwin's felt obligated to invite her for dinner and complied with her request, but twenty years later they still recall the incident with some resentment, feeling that they had been taken advantage of by a woman who was a skillful interloper/freeloader.

The following encounter illustrates how a targeted hostess remained resolute and refused to be intimidated.

George's mother from Michigan was visiting her son and his family in Florida. Her sister lived in a suburb of Miami close to George's home, and she had been invited to spend a few days there. George didn't just drop his mother off at her sister's, he accompanied her to the door with his wife and three small boys in tow, obviously planning on an uninvited visit. Auntie, however, ushered her sister into the house and then stood outside on the porch chatting with her nephew and his wife – not inviting them in. This strong willed woman refused to be forced into the role of hostess when it wasn't her idea. Since this aunt was a perfectionist about housekeeping, she was probably avoiding having three undisciplined toddlers invade her premises. The nephew finally left with his wife and three adorable little curtain climbers. This aunt went to her grave—unforgiven because of her determined and successful decision not to be overrun by the uninvited.

OLD COUNTRY TIES THAT BIND US TO INTERLOPERS

Kari, who lives in Solana Beach, California, relates her own unnerving tale of residential poachers:

> "My husband and I came from a relatively small Norwegian village of about 1,500 people. Between the two of us we knew a lot of the people living there.
>
> One afternoon a young couple (strangers to us) from our village in Norway, were taking a year off to travel and see the world, called us to say, "Hi."
>
> They had just arrived here from Thailand. They had rented a car in San Francisco and had driven down the coast to Solana Beach. A relative or friend from the old country had given them our name.
>
> They arrived just before dinner, so we invited them to eat with us and we enjoyed having them. But, they lingered on and on, so my husband asked if they would like to stay for the night. We had two empty beds with clean sheets and they were very grateful for the offer.
>
> Well, that one night invitation turned into a two weeks stay. They left every morning after a good breakfast, and went around to all the sights here in San Diego. But what really got me was how they could time it to come back home exactly as dinner was ready. I love cooking for people, but I do not like being used."

It appears that these interlopers were intent on staying with Kari and her husband when they stepped through the door to say "Hi." When it became obvious that the interlopers were lingering, Kari or her husband could have stood to indicate the visit was over and said, "It was nice to meet you. Let us know where you are staying and perhaps we can meet somewhere for a drink before you return to Norway." This couple was adept at playing the hospitality entitlement chord. It worked.

DEFENSIVE TACTICS FOR DINNER TIME DROP-INS

Often interlopers are friends or relatives that simply show up at dinner time in search of a free meal.

There was an elegant friend of mine who arrived at dinner time every Tuesday. Finally, I stopped cooking and simply opened a bottle of wine and served a few cheese crackers. A couple of weeks into wine and cheese crackers, she asked why I had stopped preparing dinner for her. My response was that I no longer ate dinner. I was quickly dropped from her social list. The suspicion is that she had regular dinner stops around town throughout the week.

Another couple who often found they were feeding chronic dinnertime invaders finally hit upon a plan to rid themselves of these intruders.

After serving the uninvited "guests" a very nice dinner, the hostess asked the female visitor to help her pick up the plates and take them to the kitchen. The guest responded and was directed to just put the dishes on the kitchen floor. Whereupon the hostess called in her dogs; Daisy and Isobel promptly licked the plates clean. The hostess then picked up the dishes and put them in the cupboard.

What a creative, dramatic and entertaining approach to problem solving! I'll admit, this sounds like an urban myth, but, the lovely housewife who shared this story swears it is true. It might have been better if the invaded family had simply met these interlopers/freeloaders at the door with a logical reason for not inviting them into the house. They might have said: "You have caught us at a poor time. Next time, please remember to call before you plan to visit." If the family actually wanted to spend time that evening with the uninvited, they might have enthusiastically invited them in, poured them a drink and left them in the living room telling them that they were in the middle of dinner and would join them when they were finished. Additional excuses and explanations are not necessary.

June and Harry always felt defenseless when friends frequently appeared as dinner-time drop-ins. Finally, one evening when they answered the door, they declared how happy they were to see them, but they had another dinner invitation. They then gave the interlopers a drink, grabbed their coats, shooed the undesirables out the door. Harry and June drove themselves around the neighborhood until the coast was clear. Ever after, they refused to answer the door at dinnertime and screened all of their calls — dropping these moochers from their social list.

DEALING WITH CHEAPSKATES

It needs to be made clear that it is not the role of the host to finance the guest's vacation.

After moving from Washington, D.C. to Kentucky, Jim and Barbara were frequently visited by their former neighbors, Doug and Sandra. Jim and Barbara found themselves not only providing free room and board for their former neighbor's vacation, but when they would go out to dinner, Doug would vanish to the men's room just before the check arrived. Since this happened several times, Jim needed to wise up and request separate checks before ordering the meal, or at some point simply tell Doug "I'll 'let' you have the check this time". Whether it is an ego issue, ingrained manners, or cowardice, some men also suffer with Advanced Doormat Syndrome. These guys are fair game for those afflicted with Mega-Moocher Syndrome. Doug and Sandra were true free-loaders. By virtue of their houseguest status, they owed Barbara and Jim a minimum of a fine dinner at an upscale restaurant. Because the old adage, "Fool me once, shame on you, fool me twice, shame on me," applies here, Jim and Barbara needed a ready excuse for refusing to entertain these "users" when they planned a second vacation to Kentucky.

When we are caught off guard, instead of revealing our true feelings, some of us simply revert to the built in, etiquette that surfaces from our training. Those who are mature and self-sufficient manage to plan and finance their own vacations and dinners out. Freeloading is, in fact, a perpetuating self-destructive behavior; it is a lame attempt to escape responsibility of paying for one's own vacation, meals, and entertainment responsibilities.

Marvin is a well to do business man who often entertains a brother and sister -in-law that expect him to pick up the check for every dinner out when they visit him and his wife in Sonoma, CA. The brother-in-law always orders the most expensive meal on the menu as well as the most expensive wine. Not once has this freeloader offered to pick up the check.

When I explained to Marvin that all he has to do is request separate checks before the orders are given to the waiter, it was obvious that even though he was feeling resentful, he would be uncomfortable moving beyond the entrenched expectations for him to always play the role of "Daddy Deep Pockets." It is always easy to unearth a few people who enjoy "Putting on the Ritz" when there's an "easy touch" to pick up the tab.

SMOOTH SOCIOPATHS, INTERLOPERS AND FREELOADERS

Some intrepid bold skinflints pounce on any real or perceived opportunity to visit. Mooching is their sport. It's not that these folks are lacking manners or awareness of territorial boundaries, but that they appear to have been born without a conscience or at least any real awareness of the possible discomfort of others. As Martha Stout, in her book, *The Sociopath Next Door*, points out, our conscience is our seventh sense. Some folks appear to have been born deprived of this sense. They unabashedly ignore subtle hints and social cues. The unsuspecting host unfortunately has the opportunity to study this birth anomaly up close.

Beware the folks who appear at the door uninvited with steaks and all the "fixins" in hand. These presumptuous interlopers seem generous, socially compatible, and tend to be great fun. They are often adept at providing dramatic jaw-dropping stories by way of conversation. The exaggerations and outright lies, however, quickly become apparent. Be suspicious when you are told that his niece who has a doctorate in music and performs in operas abroad singing in six different languages. He may indicate that he is the heir to some famous fortune and has the freedom to play golf six hours every day. His daughter is, of course a physician in Canada. He probably has a daughter, but she is, no doubt, a nurse's assistant.

Hosts with a conscience worry that these intrepid over-steppers will feel rejected and hurt. They needn't be fooled. The intruders have studied the behaviors of the conscience ridden, and their particular pathology may include some on the spot dramatic special effects.

If these trespassers are called on their game, they are apt to pout, spout crocodile tears, or throw a temper tantrum. They may then either slink away like a beaten dog or huff away in self-righteous umbrage. Ignore their histrionics. At the next opportunity, they will try to invade the potential host's guest quarters with nary a backward glance at the former rejection notice. They are "The Great Pretenders;" they pretend they are the host's friend, they pretend they like him, they pretend they are "special" and the host owes them, and they even pretend that they will be grateful for the gracious hospitality. Their sense of entitlement will immediately be reinvigorated at the slightest hint the host might surrender to their guile.

It's time for a revolt by those hosts who have been burned repeatedly as a result of compulsive interlopers or moochers. Sometimes the only way to withstand assault is with a firm frontal attack. Anyone who knows or suspects a person with these symptoms needs to carefully but firmly exorcise the desperado from his social group or guest list ASAP!

A Few Responses to Rebuff Determined Intruders Might be:

1. "We hadn't planned on guests, so we won't be able to invite you to stay."

2. "You caught us off guard, we have a full social agenda and there isn't time for us to entertain you. Where

are you staying? Perhaps we could get together for brunch or lunch while you are still in town."

3. "It was nice of you to think of us, but we have a busy schedule and we need our privacy. Call us when you are settled in a hotel and we will try to find a time to meet you for lunch." (Notice, they aren't being invited to the house for a meal.)

4. "We have other plans, so it is impossible for us to have you here at this time."

5. "The guest room is closed

6. "We have a rule not to have people stay here when we are away – even family."

7. "We are not prepared to entertain guests just now."

8. "We hadn't expected you and we have other plans, so lets' see if we can find a hotel so you can make reservations. If there is time, we may try to see you for brunch one day while you are in town."

9. "I'm no longer entertaining houseguests." If the person wants to know, why you've made this decision, simply reply, "it's too stressful." (Note: this is my own personal strategy.)

Above all, do not over-explain your position. You haven't invited these people; they are not invited; find a quick response to their intentions— present your position and shut up. Don't engage in debate, rebuttals, or their arguments intended to sway you.

If maintaining a sense of hospitable composure without long-term commitment is important to the targeted host, he may be able to remain polite and cordial by saying, "Nice of you to stop by. Come in and have a drink. We have a little time before we are on our way to (the social event of your choice goes here)". After a brief time, the host might stand to "let" the invaders know the visit is over.

If there is a major event in the host's family—such as a new baby, a hospitalized family member or a funeral, it is quite all right to tell folks that personal privacy is essential right now, so the house is not open for anyone to stay. Provide the names and locations of nearby hotels or motels. Hosts who find themselves in the role of hostage to uninvited guests have only themselves to blame.

There may be some who enjoy grousing about the interlopers and freeloaders impinging on their hospitality. Just continue being taken advantage of and then boring friends with how you've been blind-sided — again. If the host is seeking the adventure of an unplanned attack on his home and budget, then, by all means open the door to these folks who have all the social graces of a military tank.

-five-

RESOLUTE REFUGEES AND RE-BOUNDERS

"If you pick up a starving dog and make him prosperous, he will not bite you. This is the principal difference between a dog and a man."

Mark Twain,
Pudd'nhead Wilson's Calendar [1841]

"Refugees" are uninvited houseguests who seek to use someone else's home as a safe haven while they search for a new residence, job or lifestyle. There is no sense of vacation joy attached to these stopovers since their intent is not social and they are apt to make a deep dent in a family budget. Very often these people are also free-loaders with an extended sense of entitlement.

"Hostage" is a mild term for those of us experiencing the pinch of a "refugee" whose long term intentions are to avail himself of household privileges without contributing to the living expenses. Clear communication along with well under-stood boundaries is the only way to deal with the needy that appear incapable of taking care of themselves.

It may appear to the temporarily homeless that your house has more living space than is essential for your needs and that it would be nice if you "let" them move in until they rearrange their lives. A strong negative response is necessary to shield yourself from these entitlement seekers. "Let" these folks, who are generally lacking scruples, know that the extra room in your home represents your personal "breathing space" and you aren't prepared to have anyone occupy it.

If relatives, friends, or even strangers temporarily out of a job or a place to sleep, come scratching at your door, you may wish to duck or hide unless you have a reason to face them and turn them away from your home. People without direction — who are aiming at your residence and resources — temporarily, of course, are often troubled. Individuals who find themselves out of work, out of pocket, out of a home and even out of hope may beseech good souls with a residence to allow them to move in for a little while — until they find work, a place to live, a job — or whatever the pressing issue may be. These folks are neither typical interlopers nor wranglers. They have usually secured some sort of marginal invitation or acknowledgement by the host family that it is okay to take up residence. Because there was no invitation initiated by the host, boundaries tend to be murky. The host may wake up one day to discover that he is paying for the privilege of being held hostage in his own home. Before your accommodations become the refugees new permanent "digs," it is time to take the bull by the horns.

If you are one of the many who enjoys assisting folks because it makes you feel good to know your friends, family or acquaintances will have a better chance in life if you sacrifice for them, then you may be and easy target for those down on their luck.

Chronically helping out those who are in need has a title — Co-dependency. These folks may be a depressing influence on our lives as their irritating grumbling issues surface. We prop them up like giant puppets when they slump; we try making them dance to our music while gliding them around the floor.

But our efforts are futile; they continue dancing their own two step.

Our efforts, energy and resources devoted to help them get on their own two feet doesn't work; we shouldn't allow ourselves to be used and abused. Often these people are bold and insensitive to the discomfort of the host. Does a flea worry about making a dog uncomfortable? These refugees also tend to assume that the host's fine manners will preclude conflict or opposition to their strategy.

The prospect of allowing the refugee type to enter or re-enter your home very often results in a significant life-style change. One of my earliest experiences with unconscionable wrangling interloping refugees occurred just as I was preparing to leave on a three week trip to China.

> *The phone rang and friends, Andrew and Rhonda Bright, who had left the area a couple of years before, were calling to announce they were returning to southern California and they wanted to know if they could stay in my condominium until they found an apartment. They planned to arrive about three days after I left on my trip. I was to leave my house key with my neighbor and see them when they picked me up at the airport on my return. Of course, I imagined that the Brights would find an apartment within a week and we would resume our former friendship and life would move forward.*
>
> *Then when Andrew Bright met me at the airport three weeks later, it became apparent he didn't have enough money to get out of the airport parking lot. The next red flag went up when he said that they hadn't found an apartment yet. Back at the house, I discovered that my furniture had been re-arranged and the kitchen counter*

tops were covered with the Bright's pots and pans. Their caged parrot was squawking at the sliding glass doors and six tortoises were munching on my garden plants (To be fair, those reptiles ate the weeds too!). Note: this condominium complex had a "No pet" rule and neighbors were beginning to be concerned about the violation.

My next-door neighbor revealed that these folks arrived about an hour after I left for China. Two weeks after my return, the Brights were still in my home. It became increasingly clear that these two healthy, well-educated people had no money, no jobs, no prospects, and no plans for moving on or out of my residence. It appeared they planned to inhabit my place indefinitely.

The Brights were purportedly looking for an apartment, but nothing was good enough. I finally went into quiet determined revolt and stopped buying food and household supplies. At one point, Andrew was in the bathroom screaming, "I need toilet paper!" I did relent temporarily and give them a roll of toilet paper.

When Andrew hung up the phone after one apartment inquiry, I butted in and told him, "You and Rhonda need to rent that place. I'm not comfortable having you stay here any longer with your animals that are not allowed in this condominium complex."

My residence was a free roof over their head, with me as host paying the water, electricity, telephone and television cable bills. The Brights were refugee freeloaders with no qualms concerning the discomfort of the hostess. Finally I loaned the interloper/freeloader/refugees $200.00 so they could pay the first payment for their own apartment. Yes, I haunted them until my money *was returned. The relationship was then permanently dissolved.*

These people were motivated by a dearth of money. Rhonda's sister was cast as a villain because she refused to offer charity in the form of room, money or clothes that met with their sense of entitlement. My home was temporarily available and though I wasn't paying for their food, I was still paying all of the water electricity and phone bills. The household supplies like soap, laundry detergent and toilet paper were being depleted. I have related this in some detail to let you know that I too have played the role of doormat and allowed guests to walk all over me.

Many of us who are big hearted and conscience ridden find it difficult to refuse friends or family members. These individuals seeking sanctuary may be adults in the throes of one of life's major transitions such as divorce, a job search or relocation to our area and find themselves in need of a temporary place to live until life straightens out. Some of these folks may have returned home from college with enough troubles to make "Big Daddy or Mommy" cry. They may be friends of friends who are temporarily out of a job, transferring jobs or house hunting. Just remember —any excuse might be used that will enable them to seek refuge in your guest quarters.

Barbara and Carol were peripheral long distance business partners and Carol was relocating to Barbara's city. Barbara agreed to let Carol move into her home for a few days until she established local living quarters. A few days turned into a few months — three to be exact. Instead of house hunting, Carol spent most of her time reading in the guest room, pleading illness. She isolated herself from other family members, prepared and ate her own food – alone. Barbara eventually became uneasy about Carol's presence and finally, fed up, Barbara told her freeloading, malingering acquaintance that the house was going to be tented for fumigation so it would be a good time for her to move (rejecting all arguments). Because Barbara was firm, Carol moved.

Those seeking temporary shelter may also be the recalcitrant, out of control teenagers or young adult children of family or friends who have not yet become self sufficient. The parents of these floundering youngsters seem desperate for help with their progeny and may look for friends to provide safe haven for their offspring.

The "brilliant" eighteen year old son of Donna's cousin in Connecticut developed a drug habit and was having problems finishing high school. Donna, a teacher, volunteered to let him come out to her place in Arizona and enroll in the adult school where she was working. Sure enough, Johnny was a remarkable student, but problems quickly arose when he searched out a social life with some fellow pot smokers.

Johnny and his mother called each other daily on Donna's line. His mother called collect. He did not. Thus, Donna's phone bill was $400.00 within a three week time space.

Emotionally drained by the twisted expectations and demands on her time and hospitality, Donna simply called the airlines and purchased a one-way ticket back to Connecticut for that same day. When Johnny came out for breakfast, Donna told him that he was leaving immediately and to pack up his stuff. In addition, after putting him on the plane, she billed his unhappy father for the added expenses.

Donna's thoughts of offering this young man a chance to complete his high school education were undermined by the behavior of both the boy and his mother. Cousin Donna was cast as the bad person and after many years the family rift remains. Hopefully she learned that the role of rescuing angel is apt to leave one with tattered wings. Donna failed to establish any rules before the boy's arrival and she had no idea that his mother would prove to be so intrusive. Although it is difficult to project possible problems, it is safe to suppose that if a teen-ager or young adult is experiencing troubles at home, things won't change much by relocation.

It is the rare person who has the educational expertise, time and patience to transform an intractable teen or young adult. The host's own family, household and peace of mind are more apt than not to suffer along with the sad refugee.

Gary and his wife June agreed to provide shelter and a new stab at life for the son of Gary's school friend in Chicago.

The son, Jerry, was a recovering alcoholic. Jerry came to San Diego and found a job. Since he had no transportation, Gary generously loaned him his truck. Well, one night he began drinking again and left the truck at a friend's house. The truck was recovered, but Gary revoked the truck privilege. One day, without notice, Jerry just packed up and returned to Chicago.

But Gary and Jane allowed Jerry's brother, Ben who also had gone through substance abuse problems to take his place. Gary and June loaned Ben a bike for getting to and from his work. Things went along relatively smoothly until Ben, along with the bike, simply disappeared. Gary called his friend in Chicago because he was concerned about Ben. "No problem." was the reply from his old friend. Friend? Ben had simply flown home without a word to his host family. "Where is the bike?" It seems he had just left it by the side of the road. Amazingly, Gary found the bike exactly where the undisciplined ingrate left it.

Some of us have to make the same mistake several times before we learn to establish boundaries to protect ourselves.

Often the people in upheaval are our own adult children who have been dubbed the boomerang generation – the re-bounders who aren't quite making it on their own and have decided they need to return to the security of the family nest until they get it all figured out. Sometimes returning kids have the misbegotten view that the old homestead is their rightful place of occupancy regardless of their age.

Every now and then those who ricochet from place to place are adult children with their own kids. They are down on their luck; they can't seem to find a job, but they do know how to play the guilt strings of their beleaguered parents and are frequently at the top of the refugee status list. The "Daddy/Mommy dupes" are then dragged into believing that only heartless parents would allow their kids to join the ranks of the homeless

Glenda's youngest daughter, along with a toddler and an infant in arms, moved in with her. Glenda was soon tired of coming home from work to find the kitchen cluttered with unwashed dishes, toys strewn everywhere and damp towels tossed on beds or bathroom floors. She finally realized that although it is tough to evict your own kids, there comes a point when it's time for them to get off the couch and find a job.

There eventually arrives a juncture when the spoilers of the spoiled rotten need to cast a jaundiced eye on the limp "entitlement view" of our offspring. We need to scuttle the "provide for the down-and out" stance and review work ethic values. It takes courage to offer one's progeny a "real" opportunity to grow up and learn who they are. We might begin by giving them a list of jobs that might be available in the area: working at a packing house, planting or picking fruit and vegetables on farms across America, car wash attendant, waiter, waitress, bus boy/girl, dish washer and bell hop. If they start with the service jobs we might then suggest they share a couple of rooms with other people who are struggling to make a living. Learning to pay their own way and balance a budget are life skills usually not taught in a classroom and rarely learned as long as someone else is providing the roof overhead and paying all bills.

An adult "child" who attempts to revert to his "old room" and childhood security is issuing a plea to once again become a dependent — usually without his former "old house rules." But this is tough. Unless our children learn to find and keep a job, no matter how menial, and develop self esteem, they are apt to remain—like Peter Pan and the Lost Boys —forever children. Our main goal as parents is to assist our offspring to develop into self-respecting mature adults. This transformation will never occur if we co-depend them even unto old age. Some wise parents immediately turn "Junior's" bedroom into an office, sewing room or work-out room thus precluding a move back into his old place. Other determined parents might occasionally lend the kids money with a legal contract requiring that it be repaid with interest.

Before relinquishing the old bedroom back to your child — and there are times when this may be appropriate — it is wise to set forth house rules before the kid settles in. If the young person has the false idea that he is adult, he may think his parent's rules are obsolete. But remember, this home belongs to you, and as a refugee your child has no rights. By allowing a child posing as an adult the illusion that s/he is mature, you are assisting in truncating his development. Without the impetus to move forward into life on his own, the young person may finish life like Arthur Miller's Willie Loman (Low man) in "Death of a Salesman." Recall, Willie died without knowing who he was.

> *Jan and Jim opened their home to their daughter and a nephew after both had graduated from college and had found employment. These two slept and ate for free. Finally fed up, Jan gave them an ultimatum. "Find another place to live or in two months you begin paying rent." The nephew stayed on and paid rent, but the daughter, age twenty-six, was outraged that her mother would impose this adult responsibility on her. She went to her sister and suggested that they buy a condominium together because "I will never pay rent to my parents."*

Her sense of entitlement was, of course, amplified by her view of comfortably well-to-do parents. Jan could see that she was being used as a doormat and that allowing these young adults to continue to free-load was a disservice to their own development.

> *Brad and Lucinda allowed their son, Richard, to stay at home while they financed his college education and then law school. After he passed the bar exam and found a nice job with a law firm, he refused to move out. These generous kind parents finally wised-up and acknowledged they were sick and tired of the predatory*

malingerer they had created. At their wits end, they simply called the sheriff and had him evicted.

Pasquale, an immigrant from Italy, is a hard working plumber. He was married to a lovely Cuban woman and they had one adorable son.

Then, his mother-in-law came to visit. She stayed on and on, and then she was joined by her son. Shortly after, the brother-in-law's wife and child appeared. Pasquale found himself supporting four extra people. He would come home from work to discover that the new resident "locusts" had devoured all of the food. Finally, this hard working guy came to the realization that his home had been taken over by his wife's family. He packed up, moved out, and divorced his wife. She got the house.

Rebecca related that when she and her husband moved to the Berkeley Hills in the 70's, her husband's lab colleagues and their families poured in from Chicago for lengthy stays until they could get situated in the community.

One couple came and overstayed their welcome. They were purportedly house hunting! The wife got pregnant and had the baby; finally, after two years, the couple left. They had not contributed to the household expenses for two years! Rebecca and her husband are no longer friends with these refugee/ free loaders.

Most American homes are not equipped to support "refugees" for very long. Yet, refugee stories go on and on.

Connie and Ralph said, "Sure," when Janet asked if she could stay at their house for four or five days and sort through a few boxes before moving on to a large city at the other end of the state. The "few boxes" housed in the living room, numbered more than twenty-. The garage was also filled with Janet's things. The total process of sorting and getting ready to re-locate took two weeks. Throughout this ordeal, Janet continually down-played the number of boxes and the quantity of stuff she stored in the garage. While remaining compassionate, Connie and Ralph felt invaded and occupied. Janet was never able to acknowledge the chaos and the impact her presence had on the lives of her friends.

Another shocking instance of a family overrun by unconscionable refugees is that of Jana and Bryon Cantrell. The Cantrell's church in the southern part of their state desperately needed a new pastor. The church fathers found an acceptable temporary minister who lived in three hours north. Jana and Byron were pleased to accommodate the young family on weekends until the young man became their permanent pastor or someone else was found.

For more than two years the pastor and his family spent every weekend with Jana and Byron. They drove home for weekdays. More than two years of housing and feeding four extra people every weekend finally took its toll — even on good hearted generous hospitable Christians. These hosts were held hostage in their own home every weekend and pressed into extending hospitality for much longer than they had envisioned. Eventually they considered how to tell the refugee and his family that they couldn't stay any longer.

Finally, Jana told the minister that he needed to find his own place to live.

His response was "This arrangement suits me fine, I can go on like this forever."

Jana then explained that the church was unlikely to ever hire him as a permanent pastor until he was settled in his own house in their area. Jana then took it upon herself to find him a house — and saved his job!

It seems curious that a person who we would imagine to be trained in sensitivity and generosity could be so thoughtless and insensitive to the privacy of the family that had opened its doors to him and his family

View with suspicion those folks who are down on their luck and solicit "temporary" room and board until life takes a turn for the better. Some people are always in arrears. Open the door to these chronic migrants at your own peril. Once they are settled in your residence, the hazards are many. Their excuses for not budging are apt to be profuse and creative. It is entirely possible you will see yourself as running a half-way house or a rehabilitation clinic with no financial assistance forthcoming.

Lucy, a dental hygienist, had been divorced a year and was living in a large house with her three daughters in Palm Springs when she met Shirley, an out of work hygienist. She decided to give her a little help. She invited Shirley and her daughter to move into her home.

Lucy came home from work the day Shirley was scheduled to move in and found four U-Haul trucks parked out in front of her house. Shirley had invited another woman (with three children) to move into Lucy's residence as well! The two had packed the garage with their belongings and were re-arranging Lucy's daughter's bedrooms.

Lucy did have the presence of mind to tell them that her daughter's bedrooms belonged to her daughters alone, and her own bedroom and bathroom were

exclusively hers. She told the two women that they and their four children were welcome to camp in her two living rooms. Uncomfortable turned to miserable when Lucy learned that the second woman came armed with a paddle – intent on disciplining Lucy's children as well as her own . Although Lucy did not allow this over stepper to discipline her own children, she and her daughters did have to endure two months of chaos and discomfort before Lucy was able rid the household of these take-over artists.

The two women spent each day at Lucy's home playing cards and smoking while Lucy worked and fed the whole group.

Communication is often lacking or is only marginally effective in these situations. Host discomfort may increase as the boundaries of time, territory and provisions are ignored or deliberately transgressed. The guest takes on the characteristics of the evil Pozzo in Samuel Beckett's "Waiting for Godot," and the host becomes the leashed character, Lucky, who gets hauled back to Pozzo's empty waiting space any time he attempts to wander away or free himself.

The legacy of refugee houseguests is apt to be a busted budget, a failed marriage or an emotional lope to the other side of sanity. As a "Do-Gooder," the host is operating a non-profit establishment for which there is no tax write- off.

So what are the options if you allow yourself to become the put upon, reluctant host?

Clear precise communication is certainly the best option for maintaining an independent stance. Put your intentions in writing. Before the refugee sets foot in the house, the host family needs to set a limit for the length of the stay. You might say: "We would like to help you temporarily. We will be comfortable having you stay here for (the host determines the length of time), but you must be out of our guest room by (The host states the departure date)." If the guest isn't budging, then a confrontation accompanied by a written decree is best: "You've been here a month; you need to be gone by this time next month." "I'll help you find another place to live." "We need our privacy." "We packed your stuff and put it in the garage."

Whether the uninvited and unintended guests are Wily Wranglers, Interlopers or Refugees, the sub-intent is to hijack your guest quarters and hospitality. The host's time, territory, privacy and provisions are then held hostage until the guest departs.

Many cultures live by the creed, "The guest is lord of the house", "Hospitality is sacred", or "The guest is protected under the host's roof or tent even if he is the enemy." These hospitality standards, which historically have been almost universal, no longer resonate in the fast-paced American/global society. While we may be plagued by shimmers of guilt, it is time to change. Remember: your home is your turf. Invite only those you genuinely want to entertain and then determine the conditions of the visit as well as the length of the stay. If you are mystified as to how visitors gained access to your home, think back and review your own behavior and language. Make the necessary adjustments so you don't have to suffer through a repeat performance.

-six-

HOSTING ROMANTIC NOTIONS
AND ALL THAT JAZZ

"A book of Verses underneath the Bough,
A Jug of Wine, a Loaf of Bread — and thou
Beside me singing in the wilderness —
Oh, Wilderness were Paradise enow!

Edward FitzGerald
The Rubaiyat of Omar Khayyam

*B*eing locked in as a host or hostess hostage to a romantic figure from long ago may be the unrealized fantasy of many, but not for everyone. Miles, years and experience tend to act as transformers. Interests, lifestyles and opinions more often than not become altered and entrenched as we advance through life's many stages.

Shy retiring Rachel, who has a cozy home in the Berkeley Hills, was being relentlessly pursued by her high school boyfriend from fifty years ago. He finally wrangled an invitation. Neighbors were understandably curious about the progress of the relationship during the visit. When neighbor, Robbie, caught Rachel out watering the lawn, she asked how the visit was going. The reply was an irritated grimace. Romance had apparently vanished with the drift through years and subsequent dried-up hormones. The man was staying for two weeks and persistent in his quest; Rachel was edgy and felt intruded upon. She relished her seclusion and the old boyfriend was no longer the dream-boat of the 40's. Rachel was anxious for him to leave; she had no intention of ever again meeting up with her former suitor.

The Biblical three score and ten as an age marker for departing the planet seems to have become irrelevant in our new age of youthful pursuits and improved health care. Time, though, does take a toll on skin, muscles, bones and hormones. Fat tissue has a way of rearranging itself making droops, drapes and wrinkles the vanity plague that replaces the acne and freckles of our youth.

Take a long look in a mirror before you invite someone you no longer know for a visit. Who do you see? Are you the same person you were fifty years ago? Not only physical changes, but personality and attitude, likes/dislikes and all those years of experiences alter the former "You"! Expect anyone you invite from your past to have undergone as many changes as you have.

Beatrice, an acquaintance who works out at the YMCA, was entertaining an old beau from fifty years ago. We were sitting in the Jacuzzi when she related to me that five days was way too long for his visit. A day and a half would have been enough. She had agreed to entertain him when he called to wrangle the visit. The guy is a vegetarian, so she had to cook or find restaurants to accommodate his culinary peccadilloes. The fact that this romantic pursuer is a Quaker was also related with an irritated edge in her voice. It was apparent that their spiritual views didn't click. She is eighty–three and has no television or computer. Her idea of a "good life" is solitude, silence, and a good book.

Someone said that the search for a nurse or a purse often comes disguised as romance when advanced age creeps up on us. While the guys seem to have the advantage of testosterone shots and Viagra, the lusty wench from high school or college may have awakened one morning during her late sixties to find that her libido had loped away. Advanced age may go in search of companionship and even romance, but beware the house guest from high school or college attempting to re-ignite youthful romantic feelings.

One widowed senior citizen was in search of companionship and contacted a former classmate that he hadn't seen since long ago. He invited her for a brief visit in his luxurious condominium in Florida. When she arrived, he was taken aback by her transformation. (Note: It seems that women expect men to change and men expect old sweethearts to stay the same forever.) Disappointed in her appearance, he was further shaken by her shrill voice and embarrassed by her loud abrasive behavior when they went out for dinner. Furthermore, she was sexually insatiable (Obviously her libido was still in tact in spite of her age) and this host was neither prepared for her advances nor interested in pursuing the intimacy. He quickly decided that a week was going to be way too long. He finagled to have someone call him with a bogus story and he told his high school playmate that she was going to have to leave. She replied that she had visited with the idea that they would marry and so she would stay until he returned. He immediately bought a plane ticket back to her home town and later on declared that *it was the best $300.00 that he had ever spent. This host might be described as naïve and ungracious, but he was also clever.*

From time to time dramatic Junie appeared at Bonnie's and Gary's. She was looking for a good time and expected the Hunts to accompany her in the search for male prey at expensive dinner clubs. She would flounce into the house with her beaded and revealing gowns draped over her am.

Her final visit occurred just as Bonnie and Gary were on their way to a large pool party at a friend's house. Voluptuous blonde Junie accompanied them, donning her skimpy bikini. With bulging pulchritude, she plunged into the pool among all of the husbands. The wives, who were busying themselves in the kitchen, became alarmed, started clucking like a coop of threatened hens and proceeded to remove their husbands from the pool. They then cautioned Bonnie that Gary was alone in the pool with the vamp! An exasperated Bonnie confronted Junie. The drama queen finally stormed out of the party, packed and vanished – never again to reappear at their door.

Occasionally a friend or family member will decide that your house would be the perfect spot for their sexual assignation.

Bertha and Ben were vacationing with their two children at a mountain retreat in the San Bernardino Mountains in California. Bertha's good friend Stella called to announce that she was planning to join them for a week. Ben objected to the intrusion, but was overruled by Bertha's loyalty to Stella. Well, Stella arrived without her husband, but with her boyfriend, Sam, in tow. Her husband was at home on the east coast.

Stella and Sam were using the extra bedroom as their lover's nest, and living rent free in this vacation spot while Ben and Bertha were feeding them, paying for the utilities, and the rent on the condo. It became obvious to them that the couple wasn't planning to leave.

When an exasperated Ben finally evicted this lover's knot, Stella simply called another friend in Venice announcing her plans to visit her. The friend agreed to have Stella, but not her boyfriend.

Ah, but shortly after Stella's arrival at the new friend's place, the two of them were walking along the beach when they miraculously bumped into the boyfriend.

Apparently Stella simply moved up and down California from the home of one of her girlfriends to another—staying at each place with her boyfriend until they were thrown out.

Engaging in sexual activities while visiting as a house guest can have some awkward or even unfortunate results. I was awakened one morning at 2:00 a.m. to what sounded like someone skipping rope. "Thump, thump, thump. I thought, "Who in the world would skip rope at this hour?" Waking a little more, it finally occurred to me that the regular beat was in the guest room just above me. Good grief, I timed the action —fifteen minutes—and then a few minutes later pat, pat, pat— presumably bare-feet to the bathroom. I made a note to buy a new guest room bed. Most of us really aren't audio voyeurs and prefer not to be a party to someone else's intimate activity.

A house guest visit is defined as a stay in someone's house for overnight or longer. Some bachelors lure their girlfriends into their digs for an overnight stay for a brief sexual liaison. Then comes, "the morning after," and the possible difficulty of bidding the visitor adieu, a euphemism for, "get lost," after breakfast. Note: One bachelor acquaintance said, "Why feed them breakfast?"

Here are a couple of ideas for the macho heartthrobs:

> *"Hey sweetie, I have to leave for the gym at 7:45. The coffee is on the counter along with some muffins. Help yourself to the juice in the refrigerator. The maid should be here at 9:30 and I always stay out of her way, so you will want to be out of here before she arrives. I'll try to call so we can get together after my business trip to Paris.*
>
> *Nice night."*
>
> *Pete*

And now a hint for our female predators:

> *Hey, Hunk, Wow!*
>
> *After you've showered there is coffee made in the kitchen. Bread for toast in the cabinet above the coffee pot; butter, jam and juice in the refrigerator. I have a big day planned, so I won't have time to dawdle over breakfast. You know, luncheon with the girls after I have my nails done. Maybe we could touch base for a ski trip to Winter Park in Feb. or perhaps find theater tickets before then.*
>
> *Call when it's convenient.*
>
> *Great night! You're a dear.*
>
> *Sophie*

In other words, "Nice sexual experience, but that's it. You're outta here!"

Cohabitation in advance of wedding bells became a dilemma for Doris whose daughter had been living with her fiancé for a year before the nuptial date.

The wedding and guests were proceeding as planned, but Doris came to me wondering what she should do about the fact that the engaged couple regularly shared sleeping quarters at her house.

A fourteen year old niece was scheduled to stay at the house before the wedding and Doris was quite certain that the girl's mother would be upset that her child would be exposed to pre-nuptial cohabitation. (Never mind that the mother had been married three times!)

Doris wanted to know if she should provide separate sleeping arrangements for the engaged couple to preserve the image of the "bride as virgin" myth and maintain peace in the extended family — or what?

My advice is: this is your house and it is up to you to maintain the comfort zone for you and your immediate family. Simply inform the concerned mother that the engaged couple will be sleeping together while the fourteen year old is visiting. Let her know about the sleeping arrangements so that she can decide whether she wants her daughter to stay there under these circumstances. If not, it is up to the mother to make other plans in order to preserve the daughter's innocent view of life. By being up-front and honest, the problem lands in the mother's lap; it's hers to solve.

The opposite point of view was expressed by Roger and Lois who were furious when their son appeared with a "blonde floozy." He intended to have her spend the night in his bedroom at his parent's home. Apparently she stayed and the parents are still indignant about this episode — twenty years after the event.

It is always the prerogative of the host to decide the sleeping arrangements. The same rule applies to those who entertain homosexual couples.

Many of us would like to believe that our society has finally emerged from the dark ages and has developed an awareness and acceptance of those who are born homosexual. However, many still believe that homosexuality is a choice rather than a birth anomaly. There are many families who still cling to denial rather than admit that a relative is homosexual. Though there are many instances where people of the same sex share sleeping quarters such as in the military, professional conferences, sports clubs, resorts, and tours, this may become an uncomfortable issue when the homosexual family member and his or her partner are overnight guests of intolerant hosts.

Dave and Mike have been a couple for over twenty-five years, but most of Dave's seven siblings have ignored the facts and simply choose to ignore Mike's role in their brother's life. Several of Dave's brothers and sisters were attending a nephew's wedding in Hawaii when, over dinner one evening, someone began reminiscing/ boasting about the long lived family marriages. Dave piped up that he and Mike had been together for twenty-five years. Stony silence followed the remark.

Dave's sister-in law, Bertha, who lives in Idaho, says that she has invited her brother-in-law to bring Mike along when they visit from Michigan. Her husband, however, says that he would have a difficult time if the two men shared a bedroom. Bertha has already decided that if the two men ever accept her invitation that she will have two guest rooms ready and the couple can decide where they will sleep.

The issue of whether or not to allow unmarried couples to share the same room still arises every so often. Lodging arrangements are always at the discretion of the host. If having the unmarried share a room is at odds with the host's standards of propriety and the guests don't want separate rooms, they are free to find accommodations elsewhere. You should inform them of your preferences, if you have them, so they can plan accordingly.

There is no reason for the host's standards to be held hostage to conform to the expectations or demands of a guest.

seven

HOUSEHOLD PREPARATIONS AND PLANS

*"Method facilitates every kind of business,
and by making it easy makes it agreeable, and also successful".*

C. Simmons

*A*unt Sue in Natchez, Mississippi (age ninety-four) has her own hostess saying, "Company's coming; rake out the house!" It is up to the host to establish the boundaries for the visit with that follow-up invitation and then prepare the house in advance of the guest's arrival.

Once the invitation has been extended and accepted, it is time for an adrenaline rush that will hopefully be sustained throughout the visit. One of the great by-products of antici-pating visitors is that we begin to notice the cobwebs we've been living with including the refrigerator that needs to be cleaned. Now is the time to paint the wall and spiff up the garden "With a brush-brush here, a swish-swish there and a couple of Lah-de dah's," maybe the dingy old house will begin to look like the Merry Old Land of OZ.

Every successful business operates according to a plan. Every teacher maps out lessons. Each radio and TV show has a format. Those who entertain houseguests are no different. Attempting to cope with a house full of company without plan-ning ahead is asking for chaos and probably exhaustion. Those hosts who are on the cutting edge of entertaining know full well that most of a successful visit lies in the preparations that precede the social event. While some hosts may be adept at "winging" a houseguest visit, most of us are more comfortable if we have made advance preparations, plan a loose agenda and then create some back-up plans before the arrival of guests.

The quintessential houseguest plan encompasses safety for guests as well as hosts. Night lights are a must! They are inexpensive, easy to plug in and a necessary safety device that should be beyond mentioning.

> *Bertha and Roy were visiting their son and his family in New York over the Thanksgiving holiday. The first night there, Roy got up to make a trip to the bathroom, made a wrong turn in the dark, fell down a flight of stairs, knocked himself out and broke both wrists.*

Everyone felt terrible. However, if this had happened to an acquaintance or a distant relative, the ensuing medical bills and litigation could have taken a terrible toll on the family finances and well being.

A clean place for sleeping and bathing, a fair amount of palatable to delicious food, a background for delightful conversation and some pleasant interludes of entertainment are essential for guest comfort. The perfect visit also requires guests who appreciate the efforts extended and who also participate wholeheartedly in the planned events. By providing a safe clean setting for the visit, the host sets the stage for the dignity and respect that are central to successful entertaining.

BEDROOM BLISS

The bad joke has always been, "if you don't want guests to stay long, make sure the guest bed is wretchedly uncomfortable." Long ago, we were traveling cross country and stopped to visit relatives. The guest accommodations in their basement consisted of an ancient bed with wire springs under a very thin threadbare mattress. It was so miserable, that I finally ended up sleeping on the concrete floor. My husband and I cut the visit short. Saving a few bucks on a motel bill wasn't worth suffering with a crippled back.

It is the obligation of the host to make sure the guest room bed has clean sheets. For those hosts who are inundated with an inordinate number of guests and are caught up in the revolving door or "hot sheets" syndrome, it is certainly acceptable to have the linens available for the guests to make up their own beds and hang their own towels.

Jan often goes to visit her friend in another part of the county, and since she knows the whereabouts of the linen closet, she simply makes up her own bed and then the following morning strips the bed and takes the linens to the laundry area.

On occasion, the host may have a schedule that precludes preparing thoroughly for houseguests. If the host senses that the visit involves too many demanding chores and too little time to do them, it is perfectly fine to tell the guest he will have to fend for himself. The host can say: "There wasn't time for me to make up the bed or make any 'real' plans in advance, so I am going to 'let' you take care of some of the chores and we can plan activities as we move along." Some guests will undoubtedly feel comfortable when the host deliberately leaves a couple of household tasks undone, allowing him to assist in doing them. Certainly, many guests enjoy helping with shared work. "Whistle (or talk) while you work."

Along with fresh linens and towels, the ideal guest room should have readily available extra blankets, a closet with several hangers, a couple of empty cabinet drawers, a chair along with one of those folding racks for a suitcase, and a nightlight. The closet might also contain some clean flip flops or slippers and a clean (one size fits all) robe. A reading lamp along with some magazines or books that might be of interest to the guest is a thoughtful gesture. A small basket with bottled water and juice, a couple of apples, small packages of cookies and granola bars or tiny candy treats will assure guests that midnight or between meal snacks are there for the taking. Kids love the basket treats; it's kind of like Easter for them.

I have learned the hard way never to give up my bed for guests. Provide the most comfortable sleeping arrangements possible if you have company, but don't give up your bed. There is enough stress with guests in the home without losing sleep and your turf as well.

When I asked Jamina, the receptionist in my dentist's office, if she ever had house guests, she rolled her eyes.

She told me that her mother-in-law from Tampa visits once a year in CA, and so Jamina and her husband give up their bed for a week while she is in their home. The couple sleeps on an air mattress that often leaks air, so it has to be blown up over and over again. Each morning she has to sneak into her own bedroom for her work clothes and to take a shower in her own bathroom. Jamina has two teenage daughters. Their bathroom is totally untidy and the counter resembles a cluttered make-up boutique — unfit for use by either grandma or even mom.

Jamina did say that she likes her mother-in-law and that she pitches in to help make meals and helps clean up, so forgoing her bed and privacy for a week is a small sacrifice that she makes willingly.

Vicki was beside herself with indecision. Her daughter, son-in-law and the two children were visiting Del Mar, CA from Boston. Vicki and Jeremy have a lovely three bedroom home. The guest room has a swinging bed that her daughter and her husband didn't like. The third bedroom had no bed. Vicki was considering moving to a hotel during the visit so "the kids" could have the master bedroom. I advised her to buy a couple of those blow-up air mattresses for the floor of the third bedroom and let the whole family sleep in there. Vicki took my suggestion and before the visit was over the daughter and her husband had moved to the guest room with the swinging bed, preferring it to sleeping on the mattress on the floor.

Although sleeping quarters range from extreme elegance to make-shift accommodations, the thoughtful host should attempt to provide a comfortable clean bed. Uncomfortable accommodations with our closest relatives can cause hurt feelings. A while back, Laura paid a visit to her daughter, Annette, and her family in northern California. She shared her dilemma:

The last time I visited my daughter and her family in San Francisco, there had been a cold snap just before I arrived. They had moved the down blanket from the guest room to my grandson Jackie's bed. I had slept under one or the other of these quilts in years past, but now they looked ready for recycling. I un-tucked the quilts to make room for my feet to flop around a little, but in the night when I turned over, I got a cramp when I tried to lift the heavy pile with my legs. I don't usually sleep well the first night away from home, and being trapped under that pile didn't help.

Next morning, I made up my mind not to sleep under that uncomfortable load of history one more night. On the way back to Annette's, I stopped and bought a lovely light-weight extra warm down quilt, intending to leave it in the guestroom as a present for Annette. That night I had a great sleep, snug underneath my newly purchased quilt. However, if I left the new comforter, Annette might not have been happy at the implied comment on her hospitality. I wrestled with my conscience whether or no to leave the quilt for Annette to discover when she changed the sheets. Unwilling to risk her ire, I folded it and sneaked it into my car and took it home with me.

Sometimes just being close to our "adult" child can compensate for a less than adequate bed. I've spent plenty of time sleeping on daughters' make-shift beds and couches. When my eldest child was in college, she rented an honest to goodness shanty rather than live in the dorm. Her tiny shack in Humboldt, CA had a "beamed ceiling" that turned out to be bare rafters and walls that were tongue in groove boards with no insulation. There was a teeny tiny kitchen and an even smaller bathroom. Since there was only one real room, Diane creatively built a sleeping loft under the "beams" which was accessed by a home made wooden ladder. Cuddling in together on a mattress on top of the board floor of the loft was great fun, and actually quite comfortable.

BATHROOM BLUES

When was the last time you had to wait in line to use the bathroom, encountered an un-flushed toilet, faced a tub that had been left with a circle of scum, brushed your teeth in a bowl crusted with someone else's spit, or stepped over wet towels left on the bathroom floor? YUK! Like the March Hare, everyone's in a rush to get on to other things and bathroom issues really do get lost in the "hurry-up and get outta-here" shuffle.

Whether it is referred to as the restroom, loo, latrine, bathroom or outhouse, there almost always seem to be problems surrounding the area where we perform our most personal duties. Sanitary and fastidious matters abound. From elegant tidy sterile perfection to primitive accommodations or grungy clutter, restrooms are still concerns for both host and guest. Bathroom issues are delicate. This is the area of extreme privacy. Overstepping tacit boundaries may result in bruised feelings or worse. Even within the daily routines of one's own family, folks tread lightly when it comes to bathroom use.

The ideal arrangement is to be able to offer a house guest a private bedroom and a private bathroom, however, the reality is we often find it necessary to share a bathroom with guests. Many bathrooms have a medicine cabinet and more than one hostess has complained of guests going through their medications. This is an area of extreme privacy If you are sharing a bathroom and keep your medications in a bathroom medicine cabinet, clear them out before guests arrive. If you are a guest and need an aspirin, ask the hostess before going into a cabinet on your own.

Someone suggested filling the cabinet with marbles to dissuade the curious. The host might consider relocating any personal medications during the length of the visit.

Bathroom Necessities
1. Nightlight,
2. Rubber tub or shower mat,
3. Grab bar attached on the tub or shower wall,
4. Aluminum chair with nylon webbing set in the tub or shower if there is an elderly or invalid guest visiting

Also Include:
1. Clean towels and bath mat (with others accessible)
2. Plenty of soap
3. Extra rolls of toilet paper
4. Kleenex
5. Small sacks for disposal of sanitary napkins or tampons.
6. Toilet brush
7. Glass cleaner
8. Paper towels
9. Wastebasket
10. Matches and a candle or air freshener

Nice but not necessary to have available:
1. Shampoo and conditioner
2. Extra toothbrushes, toothpaste and mouthwash
3. Extra razors and shaving cream
4. Sample colognes

Recently I had a female houseguest for a week. One morning I walked into my own bedroom to find the guest emerging with my personal shampoo and conditioner in hand. Since this is always left on the lower part of my shower, I was taken aback (Really—Very Annoyed!). I told her that only a drop of each was necessary for a shampoo and then I asked her why she had taken my toiletries. She responded that she had failed to bring shampoo or conditioner from home. I patiently explained that there was an entire row of shampoos, conditioners and soap on the counter in plain sight in the guest bathroom. She then haughtily announced, "Well, I'll use the expensive ones." She proceeded to walk past me and out of the bedroom with my toiletries.

This woman overstepped the boundaries by entering my bathroom in the first place. Common courtesy demanded that she ask me first if I had any shampoo. She is not on my re-invite list!

PROBLEM #1
THE MESSY GUEST

Georgia and Ed. often entertained an executive friend at their condominium. Georgia was ever the perfectionist house-keeper and adept at entertaining. Through gritted teeth, they laughed about their friend whom they referred to as the "sperm whale." It seems that every time he left the bathroom the entire place was wet — ankle deep in water and steamed mirrors. Apparently he showered, shaved, splashed and left puddles everywhere along with wet towels dumped on the floor.

PROBLEM #2
GUESTS WHO HOG THE BATHROOM

We may all have at least one relative who uses this space as a reading room. As a houseguest, reading on the john while others are waiting is a huge No-No!

Naomi and Bill invited their friends, Paul and Deanna, to spend a weekend at their cabin on the lake. When Paul and Donna arrived, they were told that there was only one bathroom and to adjust their time there so everyone could manage their personal needs. It turned out that Paul is one of those people who used the bathroom for reading the morning newspaper. He would spend a half hour at a time on the john reading the news while everyone else cooled their heels waiting to use the bathroom.

This was the last invitation Naomi and Bill extended to Paul and Deanna.

PROBLEM #3
GUESTS WHO "WET" THE SEAT

Damp toilet seats have probably been an issue since ancient times. Sometime during the 1980's the art teacher at a California Junior High posted this sign in each stall of the female faculty restroom:

"If You Sprinkle When You Tinkle
Be a Sweetie and Wipe the Seatie"

When my youngest daughter was in graduate school, she had two male roommates. These guys were —definitely the Felix and Oscar types. The meticulous Felix, a young man on his way up in the world of television, had his own bathroom, kept the house spotless and often cooked gourmet meals. Celeste, however, shared a bathroom with Oscar, an advanced art student. It seems that Oscar consistently peed on the toilet seat. She, of course, asked him nicely several times to put up the toilet seat before urinating. He, being a self-involved messy type, either didn't hear her or else ignored the pleas. Finally frustration overtook my child; she ever after wiped the toilet seat with his washcloth before sitting down. Her mistake was not telling him what she was doing. Passive aggression is a poor tool for meaningful change!

My own darling husband is a slammer and banger of doors, cabinets and toilet seats. A shock goes up my spine with the all of the dramatic clanking, clunking and banging. However, I bite my tongue because not once in seven years did I sit on the drops caused by poor aim. Sticky urine quickly begins to reek and represents a gagging cleaning job. I've heard the argument that the girls should lift the toilet seat in deference to the male. You lose guys. The seat is made to sit upon and up it goes for boys and then down it goes (preferably quietly) after use. Thank you.

PROBLEM #4
STOPPED-UP TOILETS

Who doesn't know you shouldn't flush sanitary napkins or tampons down your host's toilet? A toilet that runneth over is not a blessing.

CONTROLLING THE THERMOSTAT

Household temperatures may also need to be addressed. In our world of air-conditioning and central heating, we may forget that we all have our own external environmental temperature requirements. Each of us tends to be governed by an individual thermostat. Being comfortable is often a concern within a family and may become a troublesome matter when guests are on site.

One group of people being entertained at a ski resort condo found themselves tiptoeing down to turn up the heat during the night. The guests were freezing and the blankets were inadequate. Lo! The following morning they learned that their host had made the thermostat useless by completely turning off the heat! Everyone laughed about it after the fact, but it was a miserable experience at the time. The host was responsible, in this case, for supplying plenty of extra blankets or else to have left the thermostat at a reasonable temperature.

The opposite problem arose for guests in a desert climate where the host had learned to adapt to fluctuating temperatures without air-conditioning. He broke out the fans only when temperatures rose above 100 degrees. Guests were in a sweat!

Since we live in a cool spot close to the ocean, it isn't necessary for us to have air conditioning. When I was expecting house guests last summer, I bought two inexpensive fans for the guest rooms just in case the temperature rose above our guest's comfort zone.

THE GRAND ENTRANCE AND OTHER RESIDENTIAL ISSUES

The house entryway probably needs to have a few umbrellas and a place for overshoes if you live in a climate where they are required. Hosts who insist that folks remove their shoes before treading on the carpet, rugs or main floor of the house should keep a basket of clean rolled socks is in order. Even the cleanest feet exude oils and odors that stick to carpets and floors. At the door — or just outside the door—provisions should be made to shed snow, mud or sand before entering.

One house guest chronically irked her hostess by going to the beach and tracking in sand without thinking about scratching hardwood floors, leaving sand in white carpet, or considering the extra work of vacuuming up

the mess. In this case, the hostess needed to firmly ask
that the guest remove the sand with a hose or damp towel
before entering the house.

This is especially important if you live near a beach. Guests, especially children, may not realize how much sand a body can drag in. An outdoor shower area, if it exists, or even a garden hose, should be available to guests. At that time, explain why they need to use it.

Be sure to point out the squeaky stair, scraping/ banging door or window sash, a difficult to flush toilet, the likelihood of a cold shower if more that one faucet is running, a problem with the clothes dryer or the innumerable other minor noisy or irritating quirks in your home that might unsettle guests if they aren't forewarned. Those Twenty-Something's need to be told about the third stair from the top that squeaks and is apt to wake the household if stepped on at 3:00 a.m.

A lovely lady who frequently entertains houseguests also has a guest book that she asks folks to sign, and write a note, or for little folks, draw a picture, telling about their stay in her home. This book is full of delightful expressions of gratitude. It is a diary of thank you notes and a remembrance of happy past events. This woman also has two rules for her houseguests: Always turn on the security alarm when leaving the house— even to walk around the block, and never ever leave a door open "so the cats can get out."

Because the Thompson's have so many people who stay at their home when they are out of town, Stephanie created a list of household Do's and Don'ts for guests. Her list reads like this:

Dear _____

Welcome! Sorry to miss you. Help yourself if you need something.

1. Clothes rack in exercise room — ask Bonnie, our housekeeper, for more hangers.

2. Towels, blankets in hall closet.

3. Feel free to use pool. Jacuzzi is too complicated to explain, please don't use it. Sorry about that. Okay to use treadmill.

4. If grass turns brown, please water by hand; call Bruce at (618)437-2240 to fix the sprinkler if it isn't working.

5. If you want a <u>great</u> massage, call Robert (618)355-2513. He charges -$45 - $50/hour. He'll work on short notice (1/2 hour) at 8 or 9 at night. Say you're my relative.

6. All our phones are 618 area code. Kitchen, corner coffee table and computer room – Lou's line is (618)362-2111 My office phone is on the floor. There is a phone on the stereo speaker, and a beige phone in the computer room – my line is (618)363-3321.

7. 2 space heaters in basement – bring up if cold.

8. Emergency #'s on the side of the fridge; for house problems, call handyman, Bill, immediately.

9. My friend Valerie Wallis lives at 1432 Freemont; phone (618)362-2422 if you have an emergency or need help.

Stephanie also provides guest with a household check list:

Dear_____

Before leaving please double check the following:

Guest Checklist

1. Lights off – especially halogens

2. Back slider window – pinned/locked.

3. When locking back slider door, only lock top security lock – bolt too hard to use.

4. Front door locked – locks to the right – push door in with your body to lock easily. Front door is hard to open – turn knob to left.

5. Garage door – please watch until it is <u>completely</u> closed.

6. Please bring mail in and check front porch daily for packages.

7. Keep all newspapers.

8. Leave toilet lids up – Izzy the cat drinks from them.

9. If home, leave slider door open 4-5" – Izzy goes out & won't use cat door to go out, but will use it to come in if slider is closed.

10. If you need to use something or have a question, call Patricia, Lou's secretary at 362-1980. Ext 314 and she can e-mail us. Lou calls office frequently.

11. Leave our bedroom door windows and computer room door window open 4" or so for Izzy.

12. Stairwell light – turn off when not needed.

13. Circuit breakers are downstairs in laundry room by dryer – all should face in. Call Bill if you need help.

14. Water shut off in front of house on north side. (Wrench in the lower left cupboard in the garage.

These lists are models for those who allow company to stay in their homes when they are absent. You may also wish to include a list of tradesmen you use and their telephone numbers. Definitely include a plumber, an electrician, the power company, and a close neighbor who knows your home. The wise guest will read and carefully follow the household direction as a courtesy to the generous hosts and for their own comfort.

KITCHEN ETIQUETTE

Of course, the host always shares his food with his guest and eats at the same table with him. It shocks me that this should have to be mentioned, but two friends, Marion and Nina, both revealed their own distress when, on totally different occasions, their hostess, Susan, fed herself without inviting the guests to join her in the meals. Both guests were uncomfortable and dismayed at being excluded from being included at her table. Subsequently, Susan invited her friends to visit her after she moved to a nearby state. They were not prepared for a nearly empty refrigerator and no offers of any type of refreshment. The first morning when the two friends were getting ready for an excursion:

"Susan came into the bathroom with a heated breakfast roll and a steaming cup of coffee." Marion said. "I
assumed it was for me and smiled brightly. Instead
my hostess took a sip, said nothing about breakfast,
and picked up her eyeliner. That was just the start of
the awkward food issue. The next evening after a late
restaurant lunch, we decided to skip dinner and opt for
margaritas and chips at Susan's home. That didn't look
promising when Susan started examining her digital
photos on her computer and chomping on the tortilla
chips I had brought. In desperation, I started foraging
for a snack in the kitchen. Then, Susan did the inex-
plicable. She came into the kitchen, looked at me and
turned off the light. 'I want to look at the stars from the
deck outside.' Susan explained. There I was, standing in
the dark, hungry and annoyed."

Unfortunately, another teacher friend, Nina, who had
known Susan for many years and helped move her to the desert,
had a similar experience when invited for a visit after the new
house was in order.

Nina had been out on the deck watching the sunset.
She sensed it was dinner time and went into the house.
There Nina found Susan, her hostess, eating dinner —
alone. It is, of course, unusual to encounter a hostess
so self-involved that she would fail to meet the basic
minimal expectations of invited guests.

An invited guest's basic needs should be fulfilled. A guest
depends on the hostess for sustenance and when food isn't
readily offered, not much else matters.

After experiencing a severe stretch of hunger pains while
visiting friends, I always tuck some Power bars into my suitcase.

In this instance, we had been treated to a nice brunch around 10:00 A.M., visited some interesting local attractions and then there was no food until dinner at 8:00 P.M. I thought I was going to faint! As a result of this experience, I always bake cookies before company arrives. I also load up the refrigerator with nice cheeses and made- ahead appetizers that can tone down hunger pangs between meals.

It is best if menus include some food prepared and ready in advance of the visit. Even people who enjoy creating al fresco in the kitchen, usually prefer to have some meals in the freezer and ready to go. You will be able to relax and enjoy your company if you don't have to always engage in frenzied meal preparation.

In years past, the female member of the family was expected to cook all, serve all and clean up all. Things have changed. Lunches and dinners that are eaten at home may come from the freezer section of any grocery store or the prepared food section of any number of Big Box stores. Though many of us enjoy cooking most of our meals from scratch, when house-guests are around for three or more days, it is often impractical to juggle all of the chores, conversation and entertainment without losing balance, patience and good humor.

Ginny B. always stocks the kitchen and refrigerator with muffins, bagels, juice, yogurt, sandwich meat, and bread along with plenty of veggies and dressing for salads. She then tells her guests to pretend they live there. Ginny leaves for the gym early each morning and she doesn't alter her routine for guests. By the same token, guests are free to sleep in or get up whenever they wish. Ginny isn't fond of cooking, so she provides dinner only a couple of nights when guests are there; the rest of the time, they eat out. Most guests are probably more comfortable with this casual approach to being entertained and it certainly removes much of the stress from the host.

TRANSPORTATION AND ENTERTAINMENT PLANS

If your guest will be renting a car, you may wish to provide the name and address of a car rental agency near your home. We have learned, however, that it is much more comfortable if visitors arriving by plane pick up their rental car at the airport. Providing information about other available transportation such as trains, busses, or trolleys in the area is an important courtesy.

SCHEDULED EVENTS

It is presumed that the host and guest will have exchanged some ideas about planned events and entertainment opportunities during the visit. If this issue is somewhat up in the air, the host might want to stop by the local Chamber of Commerce, Tourist Information Center, or a motel lobby and pick up brochures for excursions in the area. Every area of the country has museums and sports attractions as well as local events. Have these brochures available to discuss with the guests upon their arrival.

Phil has a lovely beach home just north of Rio de Janeiro. Relatives of his ex-wife asked if they could visit him while he was there, and he welcomed their self-invitation. Once they arrived, however, it became apparent that they expected him to chauffeur them around Brazil. He bluntly told them that he spent his time there working on the beach and if they wanted to see Brazil, they would

*have to hire a car for local sightseeing and maybe take
air transportation to more distant places. The guests
complied with his suggestions and enjoyed a wonderful
vacation.*

It is quite possible that the host has no interest in seeing
his own local sights for the umpteenth time and will expect the
guest to take charge of his own sightseeing tours using his own
car. Daily trips should be planned, so guests will know when to
be back at the house for meals or other shared activities.

*Carol said that when she moved to Hawaii she was
inundated with company. When the third set of houseguests arrived, she told them that they would have to rent
a car. She had other things to do and besides, she had
been around the island enough and had no interest in
re-visiting the Pearl Harbor Memorial.*

During one especially enjoyable visit with friends in another
state, my hosts took me to a delightful musical put on by the
students at the local high school. The hostess also took me to
the local high school English class where the students had made
special projects. During this same visit, these gracious hosts
took me to the home (now a museum) of a famous author who
lived and wrote in the area.

It is usually frustrating for the host who has offered his
home so visitors can have the tourist sights and planned events
and then have them refuse or be too lazy to participate.

Several years ago, we invited a family of four from Canada to
visit us for two weeks at our home in southern California. This
two week invitation was offered because we thought a family
with children ages five and eight would need the time to visit the
many attractions in San Diego.But they refused to budge from
the television where they lodged themselves and ate the full two

weeks. At one point my husband insisted that the father, a relative of his, take his family up to visit the Wild Animal Park that was an hour drive from our house. They left and we breathed a sigh of relief — grateful for a bit of space. They returned in no time at all because when they arrived at the ticket window, they decided that the park was too expensive.

This disastrous visit was partially my fault. I should have told this family we were expecting them to take their children to the zoo, parks and museums. I should have sent them brochures which included the costs to visit these attractions. Of course, I could not have guaranteed a different outcome, but at least they would have known what to expect.

Another time we entertained a newly widowed guest for an overnight visit. We planned on a visit to a museum with a special exhibit of a universal theme that all humanity should appreciate. Before we told him the trip to the museum was cancelled because of bad weather he said, "If you plan on going to a museum, you can go and I'll stay home." His idea of great entertainment is to sit around and drink and talk about how successful he was in business. We understand that he is still in crisis. We are aware that we can't do life for someone else. We are, however, reluctant to entertain those who have little or no curiosity, interest in exploring or learning new things. Verve for life is a major element in making the visit enjoyable for all.

While we often think of the senior citizen in the role of guest, on occasion, they may play the role of host. In the following story the younger set displayed reprehensible manners in relation to their elderly hostess by making their own entertainment plans while they were visiting in her home and then deliberately not inviting her to join them and leaving her home alone.

June, age ninety, has a needle sharp mind in spite of being a bit shaky from the onset of Parkinson's disease. She is active, alert, and fun to be with. She invited two couples, friends of her son, who lives with her, to spend Thanksgiving in her lovely home in Chula Vista, CA. These people are in their fifties. The two couples spent a week with June and her son. One evening after dinner, June entered the dining room to find the two women whispering. When they saw June, they immediately stopped the undertone conversation which led June to believe they were talking about her. Whispering is beyond rude; children are usually taught this at about age four.

Still later, the two couples planned to visit some other people in the area and excluded June by saying they would come by and pick her up later to go someplace else. Her feelings were hurt again. She said that she felt as though she had been brushed aside like a little kid.

Excluding the hostess (of any age) from a group outing is unthinkable. June refuses to mention any of this to her son, but she has firmly decided that these people will not be invited to her home again. These clods deserve to be blacklisted.

If the host is aware of religious services that his guest expects to attend, it is a thoughtful gesture to have the appropriate information available.

The host family usually greets the guests either at the airport or at the door. A tentative unwritten schedule for the first few hours of the visit may initiate a comfortable free flowing stay and avoid awkward discomfort.

The male guest schlepps his own and his family's luggage. Bertha told me that her houseguest from hell experience began when the guests left their luggage at the door with the expectation that the host would heft it to their room. Apparently the visit went downhill from there.

A houseguest visit does not include free bell hop service; though my husband says that he would never think of allowing a female guest to lug her own bags up our stairs.

The host shows his guest to the guest quarters, bedroom and bathroom, then shows him where he can stash his clothes, and luggage. Then the guest is left alone to unpack and freshen up after his journey. Once the guest rejoins the family, the host offers something to drink and eat. Usually this is a cocktail and appetizers before lunch or the evening meal.

If the guest arrives before lunch, then it may be best to eat before moving on to a local tourist attraction. During drinks and lunch, the host and guest can together create the agenda for the remainder of the visit.

Though those of us who entertain would like to extend the amenities found only in an upscale four star hotel, most of us simply don't live like that, and besides, this is a house guest visit. Private folks are not in the habit of providing free hotel accommodations and most of us resent the attitude of, "Here we are, aren't you lucky; now provide us with the lifestyle to which we would like to become accustomed."

The house guest invitation does not represent the opportunity for the invited to indulge himself in a free vacation provided by family, friend or acquaintance.

The host/ess is expected to prepare the house for the comfort of guest and family without feeling s/he is held hostage to an inordinate amount of extra housework.

Planning for everyone to have some space and time alone is essential for any successful house guest visit. Three or four days of non-stop conversation or entertainment is unreasonable for everyone involved. The guest needs to bring along a book for those times when the host is otherwise engaged. The host needs to provide space and opportunity for the guest to be alone to nap or read.

PREPARING FOR MEDICAL EMERGENCIES

The word "entertaining" suggests a happy encounter and though we haven't taken a vow, the good health of both host and guest is implied. Medical emergencies may arise, however, and everyone involved should be prepared. If we are traveling with a tour group or are guests on a cruise line, filling out medical information is part of the plan and procedure before departing. Guests should carry with them a list of their medications and the phone numbers of close family or emergency contacts including their doctor. The guest needs to take care of his own medical expenses.

If the host should fall ill, the guest needs to assess the situation, and if he senses he is in any way going to make the situation more awkward or uncomfortable, he needs to diplomatically, depart.

It would be comforting to think that no one would have the temerity to die while visiting as a house guest, but it has happened.

Steve, an ageing bachelor, was visiting friends from his days in the Navy. He went to bed hale and hearty, but failed to appear for breakfast. When the host checked his room, Steve had died of a heart attack in his sleep.

The shock of such an event occurring to a guest is unthinkable, but we need to know what to do if such a thing happens. My first impulse would to be to call 911. After the emergency team and coroner have been contacted, obviously, the closest relatives need to be alerted to the tragedy.

-eight-

HOSPITALITY DOESN'T INCLUDE THE KEYS!

"Hope tells a flattering tale,
delusive, vain, and hollow."

Wrother

We set ourselves up to be held hostage when we lend the keys of our home or automobile to guests. Keys are personal tools of ownership designed to protect our safety and privacy. Of course, we should only lend them to people we trust and it is apt to come as a shock when even these people overstep boundaries. When a host becomes uneasy about having temporarily loaned out his keys, recovering them may be awkward and require major diplomatic skills or even subterfuge.

HOUSE KEYS SHOULD BE AVAILABLE ONLY TO THOSE
WHO ARE THE LONG TERM IMMEDIATE OCCUPANTS
OF THE HOUSEHOLD.

I made the mistake of telling a nephew, who was stationed in the military nearby, where I hide my extra house key. I thought that he would call and let me know before he planned a visit. Apparently his understanding was that he could avail himself of my hospitality any time he felt like it. One evening I arrived home to find that he had come to my home and simply let himself in without forewarning. I was furious with myself for not protecting my own privacy.

Teresa who has a large home and entertains many house guests said that she couldn't believe how often she has had to write departed guests asking them to return her house key.

When it is necessary to provide guests with a key, consider putting the key in one of those magnetic containers and hiding it in a convenient place. Ask the guest to replace the key each time it is used. After the guests leave, move the key to a new place. Apartment or condominium dwellers may need to find other solutions for allowing guests to enter the home on their own and then secure the premises after they leave.

Phyllis was visiting friends. Her hosts had left for work before she was out of bed. Upon arising, Phyllis put on her bathrobe and padded out to pick up the morning paper — and locked herself out of the house! Her hosts hadn't provided her with the whereabouts of a hidden key, and there was no way to regain entrance to the house. Phyllis went from door to door in the neighborhood wearing only her bathrobe until she found a neighbor who was able to help her contact her hosts.

Providing a house key even to friends, may leave us with some concerns about privacy and security.

Janet reported that she had given a visiting friend a house key. Without her permission, he took it upon himself to have another key made. It was then very difficult for her to retrieve the extra key. During a return visit, she gave him the garage door opener to use as a temporary mode of accessing the house when she wasn't there, eliminating the need for a key. *After the first experience, some of us would have been suspicious and placed him on the "Do not invite" list.*

Bernard and Susan White married late in life. They moved into Bernard's large home, planning to live happily ever after. The only problem was that Bernard's daughter still had keys to the residence and felt she was entitled to use the residence at will.

While they were off on a cruise, Bernard's adult daughter, without invitation or permission, appropriated Daddy's home for a week's vacation. She also invited twelve friends to join her for a romp in the residence. Upon their return from the cruise, Susan was livid to learn that her stepdaughter had used the master bedroom, gone through her closets and drawers, enjoyed the use of the pool and Jacuzzi and left the kitchen a mess.

This daughter, in spite of the fact that she was married and had a child, obviously considered her daddy's home hers and viewed the stepmother as an interloper. She couldn't understand the resulting pow-wow regarding what she considered her privileges.

Kay planned to meet with family members for a wedding in Los Angeles. Her nephew called to say that he and his wife would see her at the wedding and then would ride down to San Diego with her afterwards. Kay asked him what he planned to do for transportation during the stay. The response was, "We will use your car."

He was not only wrangling an invitation, but also intending to use her car during the visit.

She replied with, "I have a company car and you don't work for my company."

His rejoinder was, "You can drive us around San Diego."

Kay's answer to that was, "Since I work, that won't be possible."

The wranglers then decided, "We'll just hang out at your pool."

Kay then had to tell them that her condominium pool was restricted to owners and they wouldn't be able to use it unless she was there.

Finally these determined wily wranglers rented their own car and the visit continued comfortably within Kay's boundaries.

Kay had no intention of being blindsided. Hooray for her forceful communication skills! They didn't get her car, but they did succeed in getting a "rent-free" holiday without an invitation from Kay!

Rhonda and Raymond Bonhause live in Carlsbad, CA. They spend every summer in their second home at Houghton Lake, Michigan.

One summer they agreed to let a niece from Arizona to stay at the house while she was taking a class at UCSD. They gave her a key that she never returned.

Not long after this, the niece asked if her family could stay at the house for a brief vacation. This wasn't a problem, but the visits continued, and were sometimes inconvenient. The sense of entitlement began to rankle when the host noticed that the niece and her family stored personal items in the garage – obviously anticipating return visits. Sometimes they arrived at the Bonhause residence sans an invitation or advance notice.

The Bonhause's, tired of playing the pushover role, decided to regain control of their privacy by mailing the stored items back to Arizona. Then they had the locks for the house changed!

Unexpectedly long phone bills that arrive a month or so after the company has left may be a problem with lending keys to people who are not members of the immediate family. Though we all want to believe that our guests are trustworthy, securing the phone by cutting off long distance service or limiting its use through the phone company may be a wise move. It is far better to be cautious than receive a nasty shock when the phone bill arrives and then face the need to confront the person who has abused your hospitality.

I am also very touchy about anyone outside my family using my computer. We have a lot of private information on our computer and so I refuse to allow guests to use it. If I were away when guests were staying at the house, I would have the computer disengaged or simply have a deadbolt lock put on the office door. If guests feel they need to use a computer, they can go down to the local juice shop or postal outlet; both have computer services for rent.

In the same vein, we prefer that guests not tie up the phone line by plugging in heir own computer. Once again, "Boorish Bob" conducted his personal business via his computer when we weren't out gallivanting; As a result, we were often unable to call out or receive calls. He seemed to imagine that, as a guest, he was entitled to usurp our technological territory. Entertaining house guests doesn't mean that family business has to come to a halt.

When you invite guests, transportation needs should be settled in advance of the visit. If you are like most of us, you don't like other people driving your car. Often it is simply inconvenient to have another person borrow your transportation and in this age of advancing gas prices, the subject becomes even touchier.

> *Beth's brother, Michael, from Ireland, visits her for six weeks every year. He is a priest and says mass at a church two miles from Beth's house. For several years, Michael shared Beth's automobile. Though sometimes Father. Michael would walk to the church, often he would take the car or have Beth take him there and pick him up after the service. Beth enjoys having her brother visit, but she began to feel burdened and resentful about having to play chauffeur or share her car and revise her own routine. They finally came to an agreement and Michael now rents a car for the duration of his vacation with Beth.*

In order to avoid the inconvenience of lending your vehicle, simply say, "We don't allow anyone else to drive our cars, EVER!" Houseguest stories are rife with damaged car incidents.

> *A plumber installing new fixtures at my house invited me out to see his car that had been rear-ended while his friend from Italy was driving it. The friend had no money to pay for damages, so the plumber paid the $2000.00 out of pocket rather than have his insurance premiums increased.*

It's easy to turn into a doormat when faced with a pushy guest. A couple, recently visiting us for a week, inexplicitly returned their rental car the morning of the day before they were to leave. That was when the female guest stung me. She said, "I know that you don't like people to drive your car, but I need to get my glasses fixed." She knew before she returned the rental car that her glasses needed repair. She also knew I was preoccupied preparing for a party that night.. I coulda/ shoulda said, "Why didn't you keep the rental car?" But I didn't say that and I am still infuriated that in spite of firm intentions, I allowed her to use my car. I slipped back into my built-in hospitality mode; I simply couldn't bring myself to put her on the defensive as a guest in my house. Controllers are a slippery breed; be alert to their machinations.

Nora and her husband lent their Porsche to a house-guest who is an attorney. After he left, they discovered that the dashboard had been severely cracked. He left without saying a word. I wonder what kind of a thank-you note he wrote.

Lynette's brother visits her often, but never takes her out to dinner or brings her a hostess gift.

She gave him the keys to her car during one of his visits. Though he did fill the car up with gas before he returned it, he scratched two fenders maneuvering it into the garage. He certainly didn't pay for the damage and Lynette had the car repaired, but has decided that her brother will never drive her car again.

It follows that when something is broken, the person who damages or breaks an object or dents the car, either replaces the object or pays for the damage — only usually this doesn't happen. If a guest has the privilege of driving the host's car for the duration of a visit, the car needs to be not only returned without damage, but it should be returned washed and cleaned inside and out with a full tank of gas. Lending house keys and car keys are matters for the host to decide. It is always better to err on the side of caution. It is a simple matter to tell anyone, "We don't allow anyone to drive our cars." Or "We don't give out our house keys for you to use our house whether or not we are there.

Either keep you keys securely hidden or allow house guests to access them only for emergencies — and then carefully evaluate and rank the emergency.

Darlene Dennis

-nine-

CHALLENGING CHORES

"Order is a lovely nymph, the child of beauty and wisdom;
her attendants are comfort, neatness, and activity;
her abode is the valley of happiness:
she is always to be found when sought for,
 and never appears so lovely as when
 contrasted with her opponent, disorder."

Johnson

*T*he last time that Heather's son and his wife visited, this disgruntled hostess told her son that she was sick of her daughter-in-law arriving without her legs. Her son didn't get it, so Heather explained: "In nineteen years of entertaining you as a couple, your wife has never bothered to wash a dish or in any way help out with household chores."

As clutter takes over, relationships tank. Messes that are not of the host's making give new meaning to the feeling of being held hostage in one's own home. The host may even begin to harbor a real grudge when he is required to step around the visitor's belongings strewn throughout his house. An untidy guest is apt to rank as the lowest common denominator in the hospitality status.

The mental image of a perfect visit melts away when after dinner dishes pile up and you still have tomorrow's breakfast to set up, laundry to fold and the next day's entertainment issues to address. When the host is in overload, it behooves the guest who would like to maintain a cooperative reputation to pitch in and help with the chores that are required for a family and guests to survive with an upbeat lifestyle.

The host's home usually bears no resemblance to hotel accommodations. Few of us have daily outside help to hurdle laundry and food service tasks. If your guests don't realize this, you may need to inform them of their chores beginning with their own room or sleeping quarters, making certain that the bed is made before going to breakfast.

The only folks you may wish to excuse from this are small children and possibly teenagers whose neurons are usually not yet well enough developed to know this is a requirement. In the case of small children, it is the parent's responsibility to fulfill this function. If you are expecting to entertain others during this visit, explain that you will want all parts of the house to be acceptable to these guests as well.

After three days, laundry piles up, the refrigerator is filled with leftovers and take-out containers. Floors need sweeping, dust and trash has accumulated, and dishes have probably migrated to new locations in kitchen cabinets. And yet there is still one or more or meals to plan prepare and serve. The host's nerves begin to fray — thinking chaos may be lurking around the corner. Do not despair. Remember, you are the decider! You can anticipate these problems and plan to solve them before the guests arrive.

When you are having a number of guests staying in your home for more than a day or two, it is probably a good idea to make a list of routine chores for your guests to perform in addition to making the beds before appearing for breakfast. They should fold and hang towels, and wipe up the tub/shower, sinks and the countertops. Let the guests know fresh towels are not provided every day.

One houseguest defended leaving dirty towels on the bathroom floor because "that is what is expected/ requested in a hotel." Well, I don't know any hostess who wants to run around picking up a guest's dirty towels. A reputation for being spoiled, messy, or even dirty is easy to attain and nearly impossible to shed.

Guests, part-time family and even your own child assuming the role of a student home from college, should take on the adult responsibilities and pick up, dust up, and clean up after themselves. Just remember you, the hostess, may have to tell them what to do. There may be a load or two of laundry. The guest needs to ask the host if he can help. If the time is short before going out, quickly take turns with the laundry. Folding and touch up ironing may be finished off after the day's excursions.

The guest who takes over the washing machine and dryer is another problem. Some folks insist on washing towels after every use and then running the washer only half-full. Thrifty hosts may react with irritation because their water and electricity are being wasted. If so, then it is okay to say, "Washing towels frequently is fine, but please be sure to have a full load"— or some such remark that doesn't sound critical, but let's the guests understand what is expected when using the laundry facilities.

After each meal, all need to share clearing the table, putting away leftover food, and loading the dishwasher (or washing and wiping the dishes)as well as wiping the table and countertops. And, of course, someone should sweep the floor. Done!

If the guests stay more than a few days, then the toilet brushes, dust cloth, vacuum and mop may need to come out of hiding and the host is in charge of directing the activities.

> *Joan entertained sixteen family members over the Christmas holiday. She solved the chores problem by designating duties. Everyone made his own bed. Since she had the entire family sleeping on futons on the family room floor, this was a necessity. Meals were managed by having each adult family member prepare a dish. Everyone had fun creating together; if things turned out well, it was great, and if not, it wasn't the end of the world.*

Note: Guests from heaven always leave the house cleaner than they found it. People who visit with small children must be in charge of taking care of all the sanitary and physical needs of their little ones. You may wish to designate a supply of plastic bags and an outside trash bin for them to use. In addition, you may want to give them a box to stash toys so they will be out of the way once children are finished playing with them.

One little girl was often scolded by her grandmother for leaving a trail of candy wrappers behind her,. When "caught," she began to tuck them under the sofa cushions! Even small children can, to some extent, be trained to pick up toys, wrappers and cans.

Older children and teens need to be held responsible for gathering up dirty socks, underwear and towels for laundering if they are running out of clean clothes. There does seem to be a psychological ridge (or valley) here that teens and pre-teens should tread in order to enter adulthood as responsible neat-nicks. You can make it easy for them to clear their own clutter by providing plastic sacks, boxes or other containers for separating dirty clothes and junk. Hopefully they or the adult in charge will join in helping with the task, using the opportunity to talk about cooperation while working with the youngsters.

Claire insists that her grandchildren remove their shoes when they come into the house and leave them close to the door. This is not a ploy to keep the house clean, but rather so that the kids know just where their shoes are the next time they want to go out. Claire also insists that the children eat only at the table in the kitchen and then scrape and rinse their own dishes once they are finished with a meal.

If you, as host are a step-parent, it is necessary to tread lightly. If a step-teen fails to make his bed or perform other little chores left undone that drive you nuts, go easy. Either shut the door of the bedroom to preserve your sanity, or help them with the chores as suggested earlier. Resentful teens are adept at pushing the right buttons in order to label you as the "wicked witch." This reputation is easily come by and may last forever.

The twenty-something age group often proves to be the most daunting as house guests. Somehow, they have moved through the teen years and still have trouble picking up after themselves. In fact, like Hansel and the stones, they seem to leave a trail of beer cans, food wrappers, dirty socks, sweats, or whatever they have used, and immediately become oblivious to their existence on the planet—even if it's under their feet.

One young man so thoroughly typified this behavior when visiting his father and stepmother that they cringed when he appeared. (His own sister refused to allow him visiting rights).

The strategy for dealing with this guy is to simply say. "We are going to "let" you pick up all of the stuff you have strewn around the house before the next meal or before we go out.

This young man also had a tendency to suggest outrageously expensive food that he would like for dinner including meals at lavish restaurants where his father would pick up the bill. A response to his suggestion of lobster for dinner might be: "Great idea! You go to the grocery store and buy it and then we will help you prepare dinner." When he suggests an expensive restaurant, the rejoinder might be, "Wonderful! We would love to have you treat us to dinner there. We don't usually go there because it is too expensive."

Such people — young or old need to be dealt with in a straight forward manner. This may help set them straight — or even frighten them off.

Once again, the magic operative word for the host is "Let," as in—"I'm going to 'Let' you sweep the floor, set the table, empty the trash, make your bed, pick up the towels" — or whatever the grungy issue may be.

Bonnie was (Notice the past tense here) married to Jeffrey Millington, a prominent lawyer. They restored a 7000 square foot house and a large guest house on the out skirts of Houston. The Millington's had three children together as well as three children from his previous marriage.

On weekends, Jeffrey's parents, sisters, brothers, and their brood would descend on the Millington residence.

Bonnie, ever the perfect hostess, baked bread, cooked meals, laundered swimming pool towels, and became the weekend drudge hostess. One day, she asked her husband to please mop the kitchen floor and his response was, "I didn't go to law school to mop floors." *Shortly after that, Bonnie rejected the role of hostess and took herself and the children to The Stage Coach Inn for a long weekend — leaving Jeffery to cope with his interloping family and all of the entertaining chores. Bonnie reported that ever after her rebellion, there were fewer guests to entertain.*

TERRITORIAL TAKEOVER ARTISTS

Fastidious organizers, people who exhibit a logical sequential mind set, may describe some guests. Some psychologists describe these people as anal retentive. These folks will come in and take over—reorganizing your refrigerator, kitchen cupboards, bookshelves, garage or anything that they perceive as untidy or in want of their systematic management. They are, of course, serious controllers and often prove to be intrusive and disruptive house guests. These regulators/directors need to be told, "Thank you for caring, but we are comfortable with our disarray." "Please don't rearrange the books or the refrigerator, because we will never find things again if they are too neat." Or, if you think you are in need of reorganization, you might invite them as guests and sit back and let them do their "work."

One paying house guest (roomer) who compulsively attempted to reorganize his landlady's home lost his room at her house. He would sometimes help with the gardening and then re-arranged the garden shed according to his liking. When confronted, he told her that she would be much happier with the way he had arranged her things. He was asked to leave.

It was beyond this person's ability to reform him and, he will surely suffer from his shortcomings the rest of his life.

Monica's fiancés mother came for a visit and compul-sively reorganized the kitchen and then rearranged the pantry with all of the labels on the cans facing the front. She then removed all of the little labels from the fresh fruit. She refused to join the couple on previously planned excursions, but re-planned and micro-managed the events she wanted them to attend. In a fury, Monica left the house until her fiancé's mother departed. Later, Monica broke the engagement; she felt that this woman as a mother-in-law would be a destructive factor in her life.

The lives of these controllers are usually out of control, so they attempt to re-do the lives of everyone else.

Yolanda noted that sometimes a guest may overstep bound-aries by attempting to be too helpful and she tells us:

When you are a guest at someone's home, you may want to help by paying for groceries or cooking or cleaning. While these are all nice gestures, make sure you do not overdo it. When a friend or a relative hosts me in their home, I tend to overdo helping. It was after a cousin's visit that I noticed how annoying it was to have a guest step into the host's comfort zone. So be nice, help out, but don't be helpful to the point of being a nuisance.

On occasion, a guest will want to cook a meal for the host family. Some folks (I am one) are very territorial about the kitchen, so a guest needs to be cautious about taking over any cooking chores. I may "let" them help prepare a dish or two, but menu planning is mine. Further, I am really fussy about unloading my own dishwasher and putting away the dishes. A treasure hunt for the lemon squeezer after the guests have departed is not my choice of entertainment.

Recently my husband and I entertained houseguests for a week. On the last evening we gave a large cocktail party as part of our entertainment program. I was busy all day preparing the food, table and flowers, while my husband and the guests were out shopping and gallivanting around town. Just before the party, I went upstairs to find that the guests had thrown their towels over the glass shower door and the bedspread had been placed in another room. The female guest was in her room filing her nails when I said, "I'm going to "let" you fold the towels and hang them on the bars and put the bedspread back on the bed. People will be flowing through the house and everything needs to be neat." There was no need to say more. Everything was quickly picked up and put away.

Andrea and Melvin were celebrating their son's high school graduation. They invited family from both sides to their house for a long weekend; their houseguest list numbered twenty-six and included children. Andrea allowed only wine and beer to be served in her house— no hard liquor. A half hour into the celebration, and the hard stuff appeared – infuriating the hostess as the liquor flowed.

The weekend went from bad to worse when little ones were tucked for naps into Andrea's bed without her knowledge. At one point the kitchen floor looked like Dresden after the British bombing. No one offered to pick up a broom or mop or offered to help with any other chores. Andrea announced that when their second son graduates, all relatives who care to attend the celebration will have to stay in hotels.

Certainly there are some strategies the host can initiate so that the pick-up, dust-up, sweep-up tasks may be doled out to family members and guests alike. Here's where the magic word "Let" can kick in: "I'll "let" you pick up the things you've left in the family room and then I'm going to "let" you dust the furniture while I vacuum". After dinner chores may be delegated and then rotated day by day. "I'll let you bring the dirty dishes to the kitchen and then I'll rinse the dishes and load the dishwasher."

Small children often like to be included chore activities. It gives them a sense of belonging. Before dinner, most children will reply with a smile when asked to help set the table. Since you are subtly training the child, you can say, "I'm going to 'let' you help me set the table. You may put the forks on the left side of the plate with the napkin. I'll put the knives on the right side with the blades facing the plate and then you may put the spoon next to the knife." After several experiences of setting the table together, they will know how to do it properly, and, hopefully, they will retain pleasant memories of the learning experience.

When the visit ends, expect your guests to strip the beds and take the bed linens and towels to the laundry area. Failure to comply may result in some embarrassment.

Toni shared that one time her younger brother and his wife stayed with her family for a few days. After they left, Toni was changing the bed and found a pair of bikini underwear. She called her sister-in-law to let her know that she had left a pair of her underwear. The sister-in-law giggled and revealed, "Those are your brother's."

Remember:

1. Chores need to be taken care of by both the host and guest.

2. The houseguest visit should bear little resemblance to a posh hotel stay.

3. Guests are in charge of cleaning up after their children. This includes clothes, toys, and any clutter or messes they may make.

4. Guests who are allowed to bring animals must be in full charge of their pets. They need to take care of the animal's food, water, walks, and sleeping arrangements. If there are accidents, the owner cleans up the mess. They must obtain your permission to bring a pet before they arrive. Failure to do so is not acceptable. You are perfectly within your rights to have them deliver the uninvited Fido to a doggie hotel (where someone else will "pick up his messes!)

5. Guests may help prepare meals if you invite their help.

6. As the host you are in charge of delegating chores. Don't be afraid. Remember, if you are feeling harassed, you cannot be a good hostess. It doesn't take much for a hostess to begin feeling at a loss for the comfort of her environment sans the mess of others.

-ten-

INFANTS, TODDLERS AND PRE-TEENS AS HOUSEGUESTS

"I know some poison I could drink
I've often thought I'd taste it
But mother bought it for the sink
And drinking it would waste it"

Dorothy Parker

T hank your lucky stars that infant and toddler houseguests usually arrive with their very own babysitters
— their parents! These Little Ones are precious — a
joy to watch, hug, and play with and you will delight in their
antics. Tykes are usually the focal point of a visit to grandma
and grandpas,' aunties — or whoever may be the self-elected
host. Yet, it takes real vigilance to keep up with small children
— even with pre-teens who may be may be somewhat on the
loose. Parental supervision is the key to a smooth and comfortable visit. If, for any reason, children are visiting sans their
parents, the host and hostess becomes the authority figures;
household rules need to be set down before the children visit.

Even though kids are usually accompanied by a "keeper,"
you have to prepare your home for these little darlings. This
usually leads to the safety issues.

Prepare the house and make it safe for babies and small children before your guests arrive. Some obvious safety measures

are obvious: put away sharp objects — scissors; knives; desktop accessories.

This is no time to display "treasures" — glass objects; vases; Ukrainian painted eggs — all of these should be put on the top shelves of dark closets.

Cover electrical outlets. Remove cleaning supplies and household "poisons" including bleach and laundry detergent from areas where children can easily get to them. Medications should be out of reach and out of sight. Ladders need to be in the garage — don't leave any of them set up against the house! Sharp edges on the fire place or glass table need to be bubble wrapped! It won't be photogenic, but it will be safe!

If small children will be visiting for more than a couple of days, you might consider renting a crib, highchair and playpen. You might also have a basket of age appropriate toys and books available to dole out one at a time.

WHEN CHILDREN VISIT, YOUR NUMBER ONE CONCERN MUST BE SAFETY.

Phil, a safety engineer, declared that "Kids devise amazing ways to kill themselves." He then went on to tell about the time he discovered his own four year old brandishing a large butcher knife in the kitchen—chop chop — chop chop. The little girl ignored his pleas to "Give daddy the knife," and it took his wife a very long time before she was able to distract the child and side-step the peril.

With much embarrassment, I relate the time I told my own four year old to "Get lost," because I was finishing a paper for a graduate class. She got lost all right! The next thing I heard was the clump clump of my little one walking around on the roof.

We had left a ladder propped up to the kitchen roof in order to use a plumber's snake and clean out the garbage disposal (this was done from the roof). Fortunately this adventurous preschooler was able to descend the ladder as easily as she had gone up; I was appalled by my own insensitivity and negligence. Note: A few days later I had to go up on the roof myself and play plumber. I got up there just fine and proudly did that nasty chore. Making my way down was really scary. Little Celeste stood at the bottom of the ladder and directed me to "Just throw your leg over, Mommy, and come down like Peter Pan." The magical world of children is apt to veil some astonishingly dangerous escapades.

ELECTRIC OUTLETS MUST BE COVERED DURING A VISIT OF SEVERAL DAYS OR LONGER WHEN A CHILD HAS TIME TO EXPLORE.

One little girl pulled her chair up in front of the electric outlet and slid a metal covered plastic children's knife into it. She received a nasty jolt. Through her tears, she explained she was driving the car. In her child's mind, that electrical outlet became a pretend car ignition.

Un-thought of risks for children lurk in our homes. If your residence is primarily inhabited by adults, you may fail to address the possibility of a curious crawler wiggling his way between the narrow bars of a stairwell and plunging to the floor below. It has happened. This case was reported to me by a pediatric nurse practitioner; the accident resulted in a head trauma. The baby quickly recovered, but the next time the fall could be fatal. In fact, another instance of this same type of accident was shared by another friend who is both a nurse and a grandmother.

Pamela, a nurse, was taking care of her eighteen month old grandson, Andrew. They were walking along the upstairs hall together when Pamela momentarily let go of Andrew's hand and turned close the linen closet door. In that brief instant, Andrew plunged through the 6 ½" banister guard rail opening and landed head first on the tiled first floor below. Pamela thought her precious grandson was dead. The fall had knocked the wind out of him and he was limp. A screaming call to 911 arranged for Life-flight to take Andrew to the hospital where he was treated for concussion and released. Pamela is still living with the shock of such an accident happening while her precious grandson was in her care.

The point is, these accidents can happen to those who are most aware and capable. Some older homes have built-in hazards that go unnoticed until it is too late.

IF THERE IS A DOG OR CAT IN A HOUSEHOLD WHERE A CHILD IS VISITING, THE WELFARE OF THE CHILD COMES FIRST.

Be sure the dog or cat is amenable to young visitors before introducing them to each other. An animal is territorial and may turn snappish or even vicious if it perceives its personal space has been invaded. Although some animals simply don't care for children or strangers, others are infinitely patient and kind even when hair or ears are pulled. These animals need to be protected from little guys whose neurotransmitters are not yet well enough connected to understand that an animal feels pain. We love our pets, but the kids come first, so plan for animals to be presented to little people in small supervised doses. Household animals need a comfortable fenced outdoor plot or private room, even if it's the host's bedroom, where they can be safe and protected from children.

THE CLEANING SUPPLIES STORED IN CUPBOARDS UNDER THE SINK ARE ANOTHER MAJOR SAFETY CONCERN.

Small children don't think; they just drink. Dish detergent, drain cleaners, ammonia, chlorine bleach and other poisons need to be put far from the reach curious little ones.

A mother reported that her one-year old crawler discovered and drank ant poison while visiting her stepmother who was a retired teacher. Most of us imagine that a teacher understands the need to batten the hatches and secure the cupboards when a little one is on board. Of course, a trip to the emergency room was required and could have been avoided.

SHARP OBJECTS THAT MAY BE PART AND PARCEL OF A HOME OFFICE NEED TO BE PUT OUT OF REACH OF SMALL CHILDREN.

I remember visiting the Gates family when I was a child and four year old Karen was whisked to the hospital with a spindle (A sharp spike used for holding papers) thrust three inches into her leg. This was long ago, but I imagine she was playing with it before she fell on this desk top organizer.

Scissors need to hidden away from small visitors for obvious reasons. Children using blunt-ended scissors need close supervision. Cutting approved paper projects is one thing, playing barber—usually on one's self or a younger sibling —is quite another. One three year old was supposedly napping, but was using her little scissors creatively to cut her hair; she watched her blond curls swirl around the toilet bowl as they fell from her head.

MEDICATIONS LEFT OUT ON COUNTERS TO REMIND ADULTS TO TAKE THEIR ALLOTTED DOSES DURING THE DAY ARE A DEFINITE SAFETY ISSUE WHEN CHILDREN ARE IN THE HOUSE.

Some of those pills look like candy to a kid. They need to be out of reach. Even when pills are carefully locked away, accidents can happen.

One three year old asked for food just before dinner. Mom gave her a carrot to chew until it was time to eat. A real climber, this one managed to crawl up on the bathroom sink and get into a locked medicine cabinet and then ingest a bottle of baby aspirin. That pretty much took care of that dinner hour. The three year old had to have her stomach pumped and mom was royally scolded by the doctor for feeding her a carrot that kept getting stuck in the evacuation tube.

SWIMMING POOLS AND JACUZZI'S ARE ALWAYS A WORRY WHEN CHILDREN ARE VISITING.

Parents and hosts should keep a watchful eye on the children when they are around water. Too many unfortunate pool accidents have been reported. Kids are fast. Sliding doors and backyard gates to the pool area need to be locked when not in use. Katherine is one of those parents who ignores her own kid and curls up with a magazine while visiting family. Roxanne, Katherine's sister-in-law, was understandably upset when she had to pull her eighteen month old nephew out of her pool after he fell in. The ensuing family tensions were beyond uncomfortable.

HORSES ARE ANOTHER DANGER, ESPECIALLY WHEN CITY KIDS ARE VISITING A FARM.

One summer small cousins vacationing on a farm were treated to a horseback ride. The horse, having been confined to the barn all winter, had not been ridden since the previous summer. Darlene, the nine year old city girl, was tossed up on the back of that horse by the confident strong male cousin. As soon as the owner cousin let go of the horse, the animal jolted and raced — over a rock pile back toward the barn which was a good city block away. The city girl managed to hold onto the mane (this was a bareback ride) and duck her head when the horse went through the barn door and back to his familiar stall. Mother and aunt, unable to do anything other than offer up some quick silent prayers, watched breathlessly while all of this took place —

If that girl hadn't ducked going through the barn door, this wouldn't be written.

SEXUAL PREDATORS MAY BE HIDDEN, LIKE THE PURLOINED LETTER, IN PLAIN SIGHT.

One family who rented rooms to business men working temporarily in a university town was usually confident of the veracity and propriety of their paying guests. One gentleman, however, pretended to be playful as he grabbed the family's little boy under an arm and in the crotch and tossed him above his head. He did the same with other little boys visiting the family. Friends of the family were alarmed when they noticed this behavior and they brought it into the open.

Inappropriate touching of children as well as inappropriate remarks need to be addressed immediately with the predator dismissed from the premises and/or children removed from harms way.

Such a devastating and delicate matter is usually very difficult to address. It takes a strong protective determined person to confront this problem and deal with it immediately. Intuition, sometimes commonly known as gut feeling, kicks in before solid evidence is revealed. Ignoring danger signals could prove disastrous. Watch carefully and act immediately if a child appears in any way threatened. It is reasonable and right to say something like: "picking up a child by the crotch isn't done in this house." Or, "We view remarks about personal body parts or (whatever the remark might be) to be inappropriate when you are within hearing distance of the children." Or even, "We consider some of your behaviors and remarks inappropriate. We are concerned about the welfare of our children."

After addressing this openly, it is then necessary to depart the residence with the children or to insist the offending guest leave. It is far better to have an adult offended than a child hurt or emotionally maimed for life. Detach from any personal emotional connections with the predator. As in all instances of child molestation, the authorities need to be notified.

It also needs to be noted that anyone hired to care for the children while hosts and parents go out for dinner be carefully screened or highly recommended by a trusted neighbor or friend. A male friend of mine from high school days related that he clearly remembered being sexually abused by a baby sitter at age three. He never told his parents because "it felt good." Since children do not always recognize and report a sexual encounter, it is especially important for us, as caregivers and parents, to screen anyone we leave in charge of a child.

PROTECTION AND SAFETY ARE ALWAYS THE ISSUES.

Protecting babies and toddlers is vital. The corners of sharp edged furniture need to be blunted with bubble wrap and attractive nuisances need to be removed or fenced off. Forget about decorating concerns. Clear all the tables and surfaces that can be reached of all hard edged works of art and breakables. This means candlesticks, bowls, vases, china figurines, candy dishes, heavy metal statuary and table top lamps that could topple and hurt (or worse). Even books that may be heavy and prove to be a menace, avoiding a trip to the emergency room for stitches in a little chin, not to mention possible litigation, makes it all worth the small expense and time it takes to protect a child.

From time to time, kids manifest some odd culinary habits, so unless your hobby is reading a newspaper sodden with baby spit, or a book embedded with your grandchild's first tooth marks, tuck the attractions away in your own secret hiding place.

Small children often drip, dribble, drool, leak, and spew. On occasion they have been known to circle any domicile with peanut butter and jelly or other sticky substances as finger paints; any surface will suffice as a canvas. Reupholstering is expensive. Bubble wrap is good for protecting all fabric covered furniture and maybe the floors from the kids and their accidents. Just think of all the fun everyone will have with the snap crackle and pop of the plastic protective stuff. The kids will love it—and adults—depending on their personal outlook, will find the mini Whoopee coverings either entertaining or annoying. Guests appearing to be annoyed might like to leave early.

PARENT RESPONSIBILITIES

More than one hostess has complained that when family or friends with children come to visit, parents appear to take a vacation from responsibilities for their offspring. As their hostess, you need to inform them that it is not okay to abandon responsibilities for their kids while they are guests.

Often it is the hostess who is tacitly designated the child's caretaker during the visit is grandma. Buck up, Grandma, be firm and tell your offspring that the care and feeding of their progeny is theirs — even while they are visiting the old gray work horse. (Never mind that you just had a face-lift and your hair is done in a new shade of blonde). Often grown children still see mom as the everlasting silent drudge. Give them a new view of yourself.

If parents overlook the fact that little ones have tramped in mud, or wandered into the living room with sticky fingers and used the brocade furniture as a napkin, it's time to rattle their tranquility. Of course, the hostess might first try to preserve the relationship by using the "prissy/ sweetie" approach to solving the problem. She might say, "Let's help Johnny take off those muddy shoes before we are all tracking mud through the kitchen." Someone suggested that the sticky finger matter might be somewhat resolved if the hostess keeps a damp cloth by her plate at the table to wipe off little hands before the baby moves into the rooms with stuffed furniture. Really! Where are the parents?! This kid's sticky fingers are not the responsibility of the hostess — even if she is grandma. If the parents want to sit in goo — that's just fine. Just as long as it is on the bubble wrap.

The diplomatic approach may just be a temporary option. Try saying, "I'll "*let*" you keep an eye on the children while they are playing in the backyard so they don't get hurt or dirty." If this doesn't work, tell the parents you won't be held responsible if the darlings get hurt while they are occupied elsewhere. Better yet, somehow, put it in writing. If the parents are miffed, so be it. Help them find a hotel room somewhere. It is better to have offspring leave in a huff than to be held hostage in one's own home.

In no time at all, spontaneous art work can be created by toddlers on bare walls. These little guys are normal, fast and in the initial stages of creativity. Be suspicious when little Johnny disappears and adults are able to enjoy quiet conversation without interruption.

> One two year old painted the toilet seat with a jar of his aunt's expensive face cream. Another eighteen month old toddler decided that the white wall in the stairwell was the perfect canvas for his artwork, using grandma's eyebrow pencil and lipsticks as a medium. He finished his project and then came to her saying, "ish, ish." Puzzled, she followed him and discovered that he had produced what, sure enough, looked like a fish. She got out the camera and took a picture of it before scrubbing the wall.

What the heck, if this kid is a budding Picasso, we don't want to miss having a copy of his first piece of art work. If scrubbing fails, paint will work. Getting upset is futile.

Karen tells how she dealt with a recalcitrant six year old left in her charge:

> Friends left their three young children and a teenager with us for a few days. I asked Alan who was about six at the time to take a bath and brush his teeth before bed.

His answer was that he was on vacation and didn't have to do any of it. I asked if he wanted to go to the beach again the next day, and he said, "Yes." My response was, "bath and beach or no bath and no beach." He took the bath and brushed his teeth.

It is difficult for those who have reached adulthood to recall what it was like to be a curious crawler, a frustrated terrible two year old, a sassy three year old or a non-stop questioning four year old. "Read to me" and "Help me" or "Let me do it" are early childhood phrases that can be exhausting and frustrating demands for the adult in attendance.

Avoid lecturing or scolding. These aren't your kids. Even if they are grandchildren, they are yours only to enjoy. If they are step children, step lightly; the epithet "Wicked" is easily come by and difficult to shed. Wouldn't it have been a delightful paradox if old Polonius in his list of platitudes had included, "neither a scolder nor a lecturer be?" It is for the adult who is supposedly smarter, wiser, and more cunning than the children, to manipulate the situations at hand for the peaceful and delightful enjoyment of all who are visiting.

Angela shares her recent experience with relatives and their kids:

We live in an area where the weather is sunny and warm. My husband and I both came from cold and wet regions of the country, so we often get visitors. The latest visit of the worst guests staying at our house was a nightmare.

My husband's sister brought her two kids. The youngest is going to be two and the other four in another month. The two year old is a happy go lucky guy who enjoys being with everyone, talking and seeing what's up. He is very content and a great kid. The four year old, however, missed a few discipline sessions somewhere along the way. The parents don't believe in spanking. Talking the problem through is better for the child, but it really does not always fix the problem. They do not get the point that you are mad as hell at them for the situation they have just created.

The family had been traveling six hours by car to get here. After lunch the children were put down for a much needed nap. Their mom stayed in the room for only a minute, and then she came down to join us outside. It was sure quiet upstairs which makes me nervous about what the kids might be doing, but they aren't my kids, and I assumed that they were sound asleep. Maybe thirty minutes later we heard giggling. Oh boy, now I knew there was no sleeping involved. The mom went upstairs to check on them and found that the older boy had gone through our desk (which is in the guest room) and proceeded to paint himself and his little brother with a black sharpie. He also painted his tennis shoes, my pillow, glass doors to the TV and who knows what else. We are still finding things that he had done. Even though they are relatives, she is not welcome to ever again stay here.

Angela learned the hard way that she probably should have told this young mom that she would "*let*" her stay upstairs with the boys until she was certain they were asleep. There may be another lesson for all of us here. The rooms that are assigned to children need to have dangerous items or desks with pens and black markers locked up.

Nawal who is from Somalia, shares her story which she labeled, hyper- active children on over drive."

We have a cousin whom we call "the mother from hell." On more than one occasion, she had visited my family with her children who are extremely hyperactive. This mother of four lets her children loose, never watching their activities and rough play. They jump on sofas, draw on walls, and rough up other kids in the house while she sleeps, or worse, sits around catching up on gossip. She never disciplines her children and seems to let go of her responsibilities. She is never invited back, and my sisters and I avoid her when ever she hints about coming to visit.

PARENTS OF SMALL CHILDREN NEED TO BE AWARE OF THE TOLERANCE LEVEL OF THE OLDER GENERATIONS WHEN THEY VISIT.

While grandmother gushed over the antics of her three small grandsons who were undisciplined curtain climbers, grandpa consistently came down with a case of painful shingles shortly after their arrival. The stress of noisy youngsters is often too much for the older generation, even if the little people are direct descendents and one is "supposed" to delight in their antics.

As life moves forward from one stage to the next, senior citizens tend to forget the struggles they may have experienced with their own youngsters and dub these new parents indifferent or not in control of their own family. Further, grandparents may not be geographically or emotionally close enough to be as bonded to the grandchildren as family members would like to imagine.

People taking their children to visit older folk, may need to rethink or revise the visit if the elder generation begins to sound grouchy or irritable. Instead, it might be best to stay in a nearby hotel while visiting or invite the grandparents to visit the children's home. Another option is to have everyone meet in a neutral vacation spot. Older folks have moved into a quieter time of life and often are capable of withstanding just so much animal energy before it begins to take a toll physically and emotionally.

A step-grandmother who has a large home and some household help, discovered several days after her step- daughter and son-in-law vacated the premises that the covered metal trash can in the upstairs bathroom was full to the brim with poopy diapers. These folks represent those who are either totally thoughtless or were brought up with absolutely no manners. Their kid's dirty diapers belong to them. It is just as inconvenient for you or for your household help to take care of these as it is for the parents. These folks need to get a grip on their responsibilities; your home is not a free hotel with maid service.

A similar incident occurred when Rory's brother and sister-in law visited with their two small children. The nanny who came with them left the dirty diapers in an outside covered trash can without first depositing them in a plastic bag. This is just plain thoughtless.

Candy dishes are, of course beyond discussing. These objects of temptation need to disappear before the children arrive. They are apt to become a touchy issue with the kids as well as hosts and parents. One grandma who keeps a full candy dish with wrapped chocolates on her coffee table kept hearing the clink of the top of the covered dish; she told her son to please remove the dish and put it in the china cabinet.

After her precious grandchildren left, she found a pile of candy wrappers next to the dish in the cabinet. Kids are hard to fool, so it is probably best to hide these treats before the little people arrive and then dole them out according to adult views on the dispensing of sweets.

With regard to the children getting into the cabinet without permission, please don't judge children as sneaks or snoops. Children are by nature curious. They need to learn proper manners when guests are expected or when a visit to relatives or friends is in the offing, might be the time to start that training — gently — without making the child feel guilty. The person in charge might say, "This is grandma's private place, so we don't open that cabinet, drawer, or room," or whatever is relevant. With polite training, we learn to respect the boundaries of others and preserve our own privacy as well.

FOOD FOR LITTLE ONES

Babies and toddlers need to be fed by their parents. Preparation of baby formula, juice, water and baby food —is all up to the parents. They need to arrive equipped to take care of their baby's required food intake for the duration of the visit.

If kids are old enough to sit at the table, they need to be seated next to the parent who is always in charge of getting the food from their plate to their mouth, wiping sticky fingers and supervising the operation. Of, course, children never leave the table without having mouths and fingers wiped clean.

Children who are picky eaters may be an embarrassing problem for some hostesses. Parents who insist that their children try a bit of each dish are helping their offspring on a fine path to developing cosmopolitan palates. Of course, if a child is at your table and announces that your stew, soup or salad looks like monkey vomit, it is probably best to pretend you didn't hear and let his mother handle her own kid. Depending on your rela-tionship, however, you might consider saying. "Yup, it looks like monkey vomit, but it is a delicious concoction that you might enjoy if you take a bite."

Teresa was expecting her stepdaughter, Debbie, and her children for a five day visit. She asked what the children ate, and Debbie responded with, "Whatever is set before them. If they don't want to eat it, they don't eat." This attitude made Teresa's preparations much easier. She did learn, however, that the children would only drink milk if it was laced with chocolate syrup; she gladly accommodated this quirk.

An example from the other side of the coin is that of Barbara who was entertaining a family with two little girls.

One morning she prepared the girls (ages five and eight) a lovely breakfast of ham and eggs; the girls refused to touch it, preferring a sugared cereal. While this family stayed five or six days and ate out most of the time, one evening Barbara did prepare a lovely dinner. Again, the girls both announced that they didn't like the food. The mother promptly got up and left the house returning with Kentucky Fried Chicken for the girls.

Barbara reported that these children are surviving mostly on fast food choices: batter-fried food, French fries, and breads. These two innocents appear to fit my definition of "abused and deprived" (Spoiling is child abuse and kids of today are deprived of deprivation.) These girls are being nutritionally starved as well.

When the group listening to this story was asked what their response to the situation might be, everyone was in general agreement that this family would never be invited back. Barbara's weak smile indicated that these folks were, in fact, close family and denying them hospitality was impossible. She probably needs to rethink her own efforts and stop catering to this boorish company.

Lillian had a similar experience. She was entertaining a niece and her family that wrangled an invitation.

> *The last day of the visit she out did herself preparing special breakfast of lemon poppy seed muffins, and a breakfast casserole. When the family finally congregated around the table, the ten year old wanted to know where the waffles were. Offended, Lillian told him they were in the freezer and if he wanted them, he could get them and fix them for himself. She was further annoyed that this kid had obviously snooped in her freezer because there was no other way he could have known she had frozen waffles.*

Another instance, with a different conclusion, occurred when Robin was entertaining her seven year old grandson and a family friend, David.

> *Robin gave Mark a fried egg for breakfast; he whined that he only liked scrambled eggs. David immediately picked up a fork twirled it in Marks' fried egg and said, "Now it's scrambled, eat it." Mark promptly ate the egg without another word.*

Children sometimes need a no-nonsense approach to let them know that they are not always in charge! Visiting friends and family can also be an opportunity for children to learn about different foods, menus and eating styles. Kids who early learn to taste and enjoy are apt to go on and experience lives that are richer in relationships and adventure. My own mother insisted that we take at least one bite of each food that was on the table. In later years my own daughters sometimes managed to ditch classes on the days that my English as a Second Language classes were having their potlucks because they had learned to appreciate and enjoy homemade food from around the world.

Celeste and her son, Elijah, take mini vacations to local Arab and Asian markets to taste authentic fare. Food is almost always an excellent topic as a conversation starter. We are fortunate in America; our culturally diverse society is rich in opportunities for all of us to visit ethnic restaurants of every sort. It is possible for all of us to enrich our lives by becoming culinary travelers.

When kids travel alone with dad, sometimes the dad gets a bad rap for not paying attention to details and considering the host's furniture. This was the case with Peter who brought his son, Brandon, age four, with him for a visit with old friends, the Banes.

While they were visiting, the Banes held a great Super Bowl party. Mrs. Bane put Brandon on a small metal table arrangement with his plate of spaghetti and meatballs in the kitchen, so any spills could be easily wiped up. Peter took it upon himself to re-locate his son and the plate of spaghetti to the formal dining room where the plate of spaghetti was immediately spilled on the white upholstered dining room chair. Peter simply ignored the spill and Mrs. Bane then had to leave the other guests and attempt to remove the tomato sauce from the chair.

During a houseguest visit that includes children who may be finicky eaters, it is probably wise to include age appropriate food snacks. Provide a bowl of trail mix (Don't offer this to them, just leave it out where they can dip into it.). Those rice cracker treats from the Asian grocery are also a healthy choice. Animal Sandwiches — Peanut butter and jelly will do — just use cookie cutters to make cute kid tea sandwiches. Tuck them in plastic bags and wrap the bags in a damp tea towel. They will stay fresh and ready to serve at the slightest whimper.

KEEPING THE KIDS ENTERTAINED

Toss out the toxic toys; turn off the talking furniture. Try to get in touch with your own inner child. Remember what they really want is your attention. If you are entertaining very young children, have everyone join in a parade with the leader creating the hopping, arm swinging or other physical gyrations for the others to follow. Or, just before bedtime have everyone — both young and old- get down on the floor and pretend to be different animals. If the youngest can talk, let him decide which animals everyone is pretending to be. Kids love it. One person pretends to be a kitty cat, walking around on all fours meowing, pawing or whatever, then the next person takes a turn for everyone to mimic — maybe a dog, lizard, cow, sheep — These two activities represent "real" exercise and you'll be amazed at your exhaustion and feelings of fitness after participating in this game. Entertainment that includes small children can be a delightful challenge.

Some other ideas that might help if you are expecting to entertain children are:

1. Sidewalk chalk (make a game of scrubbing it up if grandpa seems to be irked),

2. A puzzle on the side of a cardboard box (used as a table top) that can been enjoyed by everyone

and then slipped out of the way under a piece of furniture when it's not in use.

3. Coloring books. Tear out colored pages and tack them on the cardboard box art screen.

4. Small metal cars for little boys. Use the side of one of those cardboard boxes to draw roads. Make buildings out of small boxes.

5. Jump ropes (not grandma, thank you!)

6. Hula hoops

7. Remember paper dolls? I haven't seen a paper doll book in years, so this might be a slick use for all of those throw away catalogs that clog up the mailbox. Cut out the models and dress them funny. There are paper dolls out now from the American doll series.

8. Make cut-out cookies or other cookies. Kids of all ages love to help in the kitchen. Make an apron from a dishtowel and "let" them help out with clean hands.

9. Getting out of the house is important, so trips to a park or a children's museum should be included.

10. Nature walks are fun for everyone. Look for birds or flowers, collect leaves or play in the snow. Finding pictures in the clouds is another great activity—or keep a kite on hand; What is more fun than flying kites on a windy day?.

11. A Good Citizens walk was created by Jane Woulf to enjoy with her three grandchildren. She

outfitted each child with a pair of latex gloves (too big, but so what?) and each person carried a plastic grocery bag for finding and picking up trash along their hiking route. The kids loved it.

12. If the adults want to visit an art gallery, take the kids along. This is a great time to teach them to keep their hands behind their backs; choose a subject like kitties, puppies, children, blue flowers or whatever strikes their fancy for them to find in the paintings. I always let the kids stop and choose a small item from the gift shop as a memento of the day.

13. An inter-generational family talent show is another idea. Maybe even get out that box of "dress-up" costumes and clothes for singing songs, reciting poems, acting out fairy tales and other show-off fun. Again, have the camera or camcorder handy.

14. Allow each child to spend five dollars at the 99 cent store. Then each day "let" the child enjoy one of his purchases.

Entertaining children can certainly be an exhausting endeavor, but if you approach it with a positive attitude, it can become an opportunity to relive your own lost or forgotten youth. Explore with the kids.

For the simplest, most educational intergenerational entertainment, talk <u>to</u> and <u>with</u> the children. They see the world in a brand new way and their views often give adults something to talk about later.

-eleven-

TERRIFIC TEENS
A BARRACKS OF BOYS AND A
GIGGLE OF GIRLS

*"I would there were no age between ten and
three and twenty, or that youth would sleep
out the rest; for there is nothing in the
between but getting wenches with child,
wronging the ancientry, stealing, fighting."*

William Shakespeare
<u>Winter's Tale</u>
(III, iii)

TEENAGERS ARE LITTLE KIDS IN BIG BODIES.

*T*hey relish the company of their peers and often feel
more secure with same sex friends. Just as when they
were small, these boys and girls are quite capable of
entertaining themselves sometimes even with adults at close
range, but not intruding.

Every generation has its own music, games, and vernacular. Every teen generation believes that parents or adults fail
to understand the difficulties of the developmental process and
they may be right. As adults, we have loped to the other side of
hormonal surges, zits, self consciousness and curiosity typical
of ages thirteen to nineteen, gone forever is our "youth."

Teens relish the company of each other – sometimes just to "hang out." They often interact in physical ways, splashing water at the pool, tossing or hitting balls back and forth, teasing with mock hitting or pummeling. When adults encroach on their space, the interaction may dry up. When we entertain teens, we have plenty of pool, beach, and tennis equipment available. Then we join them at the beach, pool, or tennis court, but leave the teenagers in their own area.

Two teens are easier to entertain than one alone. Often the parents of an only child go in search of an extra teen to accompany them on a vacation. In the long ago, when we were fourteen, my girlfriend's parents would invite me to their lake cottage for a week. It was a great time for both of us teenagers and my presence probably allowed her parents to enjoy their own private time during the vacation.

Bryon or another boy often comes along when Elijah visits us (his grandparents), and Bryon's parents have taken Eli along to the Colorado River and to Hawaii –because it helps keep Bryon entertained. The summer that Elijah's mother was offered a rent-free chateau in the Loire Valley of France, Bryon and his mother joined them. The boys had great fun playing with the language, enjoying the food and spoofing the art at the Louver. There is no doubt that the experience was made more memorable because each teen had the other while touring castles and museums.

Since the teenage years extend from thirteen to nineteen, there is a wide spectrum of interests, developmental issues and behaviors that need to be taken into consideration while entertaining this particular group. Timeline boundaries as well as household standards need to be understood so that everyone has a clear understanding of the parameters for a safe comfortable pleasant stay. It is a wise host that lets parents know just how long their teens will be welcome visitors. Grandparents may find themselves "stuck" with teenage grandkids if the parents happen to be in the midst of a divorce, a move, or some other life altering transition.

To avoid problems, teens' eating habits need to be outlined for the host; be sure parents tell you about any food allergies or religious food restrictions in order to avoid problems. If teens need to take medications, the host needs to know what they are and when they are to be taken.

Further, visiting teenagers should have enough money to cover some of their expenses. It is up to the host to tell the parents just how much some planned entertainment would cost. Teens also need an "out" for the visit if the atmosphere in the host's home should become uncomfortable.

Parents of teenagers are responsible for the security of their offspring while away from home and they need to make plans for their well being that do not conflict with the interests of the host family.

Janet assumed that her brother and sister-in-law would be thrilled to entertain her daughter, Amanda, (age 16) for a week. Much to the host's chagrin, Janet, in order to save money, arranged for Amanda to catch a 6:00 am flight to return home. This thoughtless mother made the return trip plans without consulting with her brother or his wife who had to get up at 4:30 am to drive the teenage guest to the airport.

Safety issues are of the utmost importance while hosting teenagers. However, the danger areas for teens are somewhat different than those we worry about for small children or senior citizens.

These pubescent youngsters have their own built-in hormonal and independence issues that they may think normal, but may be at times disconcerting for a host. Teenagers are often attempt to emulate adult behavior that may in their minds symbolize adult independence.

Teens still require unobtrusive adult supervision. Often the right to drive is a symbol of autonomy and the beginning of detachment from parental control. An instance of a teen-ager overstepping driving boundaries is that of Marcie who had just earned her drivers permit. Marcie invited her best friend, Nancy to spend the night.

The girls sneaked down to the garage after Marcie's parents were asleep. Marcie decided that she would give Nancy a driving lesson. With Nancy behind the wheel of Marcie's parent's BMW sedan, Marcie began instructing her on how to back out of the garage. Nancy backed out all right! She managed to get the car out of the garage and back into the side of a car parked across the street.

Teenage drivers under the age of eighteen should never operate a vehicle with a child or another teen as a passenger; in California this is a law. In spite of this legal attempt to preserve the lives of our precious youth, newspapers still report instances when teen exuberance and the need to show off overreaches good sense and respect for the law. Once again the grim reaper destroys the tranquility of another graduating class. It is the responsibility of the adult host to be sure that underage teens do not have unauthorized access to car keys. When there is a need for several young people to travel, the designated driver must be an adult.

When teens are invited for overnight or longer, parents of the guest need to know that an adult will be on the premises to supervise activities. Some teens view smoking or drinking alcoholic beverages as a rite of entry into adulthood. Teens that smoke (anything) or drink alcoholic beverages can result in serious trouble for the host family.

One sixteen year old boy gave himself an early lesson in hospitality issues. His parents had to be out of town for a couple of days and supervision was managed by a friend in a nearby town. When the friend called to check on him, he told her that he had invited a couple of friends to come over to play video games. Well, the couple of friends told more kids that this young man was alone for the night. More teenagers showed up – some of them with alcohol.

They illegally drove into town to pick up pizza; some of the kids drank, got sick and spent the night. The next day, the young host finally had to tell some of his friends to leave because he had to clean up the house and put it back in order before his parents returned.

This is a perfect example of why it is always best to have "in house" adult supervision in order to keep kids under control and sent home in a timely manner. In some states, the owners of the home where teenagers drink alcohol, smoke marijuana or take other drugs are apt to find themselves in serious trouble with the law. If you allow a teenager to drink and drive away from your home, as host, you may be held liable if they are involved in an automobile accident. Chaperoning teens is a serious business.

Even when adults are present, unthought-of problems can occur.

It was planned that Lisa would spend a week at Katrina's home so the two eighth graders could study and walk to school together while Lisa's family moved to a new home.

The first morning, Katrina's mother served a large breakfast to the two girls and sent them off to school. A couple of hours later there was a frantic call from the Assistant Principal; Katrina was drunk! The girls had filled soda pop bottles with scotch and drank them on the way to school. Katrina's parents rarely drank, so they had no idea their daughter was getting into their supply of company liquor.

This episode was dangerous as well as shocking. The large breakfast probably helped to save Katrina's life. Alcohol in large doses is toxic. It is important to keep liquor cabinets locked when teenagers are in residence.

TEENAGERS ARE BEST KNOWN FOR THEIR VORACIOUS APPETITES!

Food choices for teens may be somewhat easier than for small children or even adults. Sometime in the 1950's pizza migrated to the United States. It has been the favorite of teens ever since – along with the very American hamburger and hotdog. If there is more than one teenager as a guest, have them make individual pizzas for the family, or let them cook their own hamburgers or hot dogs and toast marshmallows over a grill or fire pit..

Teens especially enjoy easily prepared fried apples for breakfast. Core and slice several Granny Smith apples. Heat up some butter in a frying pan; add the apples and stir until they are brown (but not mushy) and coated with the butter. Toss in a mixture of sugar and cinnamon and add a few pecans or walnuts if you like. Heat through until the sugar mixture is melted. These are great served with sausage and eggs.

One easy dessert for teens is the ever popular banana split. I lucked out and found some banana split dishes at the thrift store, but any old bowl will do. Let the teens make their own fancy sundae by splitting a banana in half. In between the two slices put one scoop each of vanilla, chocolate and strawberry ice cream. Have some chocolate and butterscotch or caramel sauce available to dribble on top of the ice cream. Then add a healthy squirt of prepared whipped cream. Finish off with chopped nuts and maraschino cherry halves. Elijah enthused that his creation looked "just like in the movies!"

HOUSEHOLD RULES AND CHORES FOR TEENS

Most teenagers are known for leaving beds unmade, "hanging" towels on the floor, and leaving shoes, dirty socks and underwear in cluttered piles along with empty chip bags and soft drink cans. Adults who have long forgotten the disorder they scattered in their own teen years may view the current jumble with ruffled feathers. Back off (this is from the former witch with the capital B). Your goal is a comfortable fun relationship with these pubescent wonders.

Get out some baskets for sorting the socks and underwear to haul to the laundry area, then either have them help make the beds (if it bothers you that much) or shut the door and enjoy the ideas of these fresh young folks who will be in charge of organizing the world after you have left the planet. These new people have a whole new vocabulary, amazing technological skills and interests along with world views that can make entertaining them an illuminating educational experience for one's self. Let them share with you and then perhaps you will have a chance to share with them some of who you are and how you managed to get from their age to where you are now.

Claire has some special rules for her visiting grandchildren. They are allowed to eat only at the table in the kitchen or the dining room (No eating in front of the television or other rooms in the house). After a meal, they are expected to take their own dishes to the sink and rinse them off. Claire then loads the dishwasher. They are also expected to pick up any of their belongings and leave the living quarters neat. She has all of the kids remove their shoes at the front door. This is not so the floor will stay clean, but rather so the kids will know where to find their shoes the next time they leave the house.

Hilda, who often entertains several grandchildren at once, says that she simply assigns team duties, so household chores are taken care of in a lively happy atmosphere.

While a house guest usually thinks of a visit as a mini-vacation, on occasion the teenager may find himself in uncomfortable circumstances. A visiting teen always needs an option to leave the host's home if he for any reason feels uneasy, senses danger, or sudden illness strikes. As a teenager, I was stuck for a long weekend at a lake cottage with a family that communicated by quarreling. It was awful and I had no way of escaping the chronic arguing.

As a twelve year old I visited a friend in another city and the second night there, I developed a terrible ear infection. Of course the family called my parents and I was hustled to the doctor the following morning.

Yet another time at age eighteen, I was in a far away state as the weekend guest at an elegant home. After Sunday dinner, everyone napped. The elder son picked me up and carried me to a bedroom. I must have screamed or made some sort of fuss because I escaped being raped and was taken back to my boarding school.

If teenagers' judge there is any sort of discomfort or danger, they need to have a number handy, so a parent or other trusted adult can pick them up. They may even have to make the call from a phone outside the house.

Entertaining teenagers can be a great joy. They are old enough to engage in meaningful conversation and share their opinions. Allowing teens to help plan menus and activities might better assure a pleasant smooth flowing visit.

Teens usually have an accelerated energy level compared to that of adults. Both girls and boys enjoy sports; swimming, boogie boarding, tennis, golf, volleyball, lobbing a basketball, sailing, and skiing as well as running and hiking. These are a few sports activities that are wholesome and fun for young people. Outline some activities that may be available in your area and let the kids decide on the agenda.

My favorite activity with teens is to gather them in the kitchen and let them do a little cooking. One summer when Elijah and Brian were thirteen, they spent two weeks here. I had them help prepare meals every day with each boy assigned a different dish for each meal. I took pictures of them while they were having fun making their creations. At the end of the summer, each thirteen year old made his own cookbook to take home and the pictures were tucked inside.

More recently these two (now age fifteen) spent the Memorial Day weekend at the Colorado River with Brian's parents. The pictures of the two boys both slathered in mud soon circulated via the internet. I'm quite sure that Brian's folks didn't initiate this game.

One mother of teenage sons said that even though the boys are fifteen and eighteen, she doesn't dare throw away the Legos. These creative plastic blocks do provide hours of fun for folks of all ages. This same mother emphasized that there is great fun to be had without employing a gadget that has to be plugged in. Note: I just caught Derrick (age 19) , who works at the YMCA counter with a Legos project in progress; he works on it between customers.

Valerie, who has two teenage girls says, "Get out the make-up and hairstyling products." Teenage girls (and many who are younger) around the world seem to have an inborn interest in beauty products. Valerie, who is a motivational coach and speaker, insists that the girls try "new looks," and critiques must be positive. Her view is that by looking at fashion magazines, girls can too often become dissatisfied with their own noses, ears, eyes, etc. Teenage years are, by nature, a time of comparing, developing and deciding who and what to become. Being comfortable with one's personal self is an important and sometimes difficult aspect of developing maturity.

Valerie also always supplies a large canvas along with acrylic paint and brushes at her front entrance. The floor beneath the canvas is protected with a mat. The girls are encouraged to paint or write something as they enter. The only rule is that it needs to be appropriate – no bad language or naughty drawings. This sounds like a nifty idea for teenage boys as well. If the kids are there for a weekend, just large sheets of brown wrapping paper and tempura paints would work.

They might also enjoy a trip to an upscale thrift shop. This can resemble a treasure hunt for costume jewelry, scarves, books, or other age appropriate precious objects. Remember to pullout the board games such as chess, monopoly and Scrabble. A jig-saw puzzle can be put on a board and stowed under a bed or sofa to be brought out for everyone to enjoy together from time to time.

If there is family time together, everyone including small children, teens and adults can enjoy a game of Charades or Pictionary. When my youngest daughter and her high school friends would gather at our house, they would get out the dictionary; each person would write an obscure word on piece of paper and then the others would guess at the definition. This provided lots of laughs and even had an educational benefit.

Betty is a neighbor who sometimes chaperones her grand-daughter's sleepovers. She says that along with word games and "talk" sessions, the girls often write their own scripts and then act them out. Just as with the teenage boys, having the girls help out with the cooking, table setting and clean-up chores may further establish a sense of belonging which is essential during these developmental years.

Entertaining teenagers is a learning opportunity for both the host family and the teen. Hosts have the opportunity to revisit their own teen years (Really, try to remember your thoughts and views at that age!). It is also a chance for the teenager to learn that other people may have different habits and live a different lifestyle than their own family. They must learn to respect the amenities of the host's home.

Visiting teenagers may also learn to develop houseguest courtesies and even bring along an appropriate gift for the host family. The gift might be something the teen has made, a plant, a bouquet of flowers, or perhaps a box of candy.

Advance preparation makes a huge difference in the enjoyment of entertaining young folks, provides an opportunity for the host to help recall one's own youth, and better appreciate the new generation.

-twelve-

TEMPESTUOUS TWENTY
SOMETHING'S

"Fortune brings in some boats that are not steered"

William Shakespere
Cymabline
(IV, iii)

*V*iola was busy working on an advanced degree at Columbia University. Although her residence was a small studio apartment, her friends from Minnesota saw it as a great opportunity for them to visit New York. No problem about the limited space; they brought sleeping bags and backpacks. Viola's hometown friends were oblivious to her need for quiet study time and personal space.

If teenagers are little kids in big bodies, folks in their twenties often don't seem much more mature. For many of them, it's just that they are of an age to travel without a chaperone, drink beer and party, party, party. Without much life experience, they tend to be unaware of the feelings and needs of others especially those of a generation or two older. These young adults may fail to realize that people in a different age bracket may have cultural and social lifestyles poles apart from their own. At times they are a huge inconvenience to a host family.

Mary Ruth and Neil (Chapter 3) who have mastered most of the art of entertaining) groups of family, wranglers, and free loaders during summers at their vacation home on a lake in Wisconsin, just reported that their organized system was shot down during this last season. It seems that their twenty year old grand daughter came to live there while working during the summer. She had two jobs and worked like a dynamo. The only problem was that she consistently left a trail of clothes from the bathroom to her bedroom, as she ate, slept and went to work — or sometimes enjoyed outings with her twenty-something friends. While these grandparents are proud of their industrious grandchild, they paid a price. Mary Ruth played the role of "maid" and did all of her granddaughter's laundry, cooking, clutter removal and cleaning.

Their grand daughter did take care of their dinner tab one evening in the restaurant where she worked as a waitress, but this young woman obviously felt entitled to a free summer residence with maid service. Unfortunately, this attitude seems to be prevalent among many twenty-something's.

Rosie has an extra home in the desert. A twenty-one year old nephew of her ex-husband called to ask if he and a friend could come to stay there for the weekend and attend a concert in a nearby community. The response was, "No problem." Rosie had invited a female friend of hers for the weekend, but a couple of young guys in the other small remaining bedroom should be just fine. Friday evening arrived and so did the nephew, then his friend, then another friend, and another — even unto the seventh friend. Rosie informed this nephew-in-name that she had expected only one other fellow and the group was both unexpected and too large. She told them that her visiting friend would be using the one other guest room, but he and his friends were welcome to sleep (they had brought sleeping bags) in the living room. The guys said that they were all proficient at the game Pac Man and they would easily arrange themselves in the small bedroom with two small beds. Aside from the under-wear hanging on the wall next to the pool the morning after the concerts, the rest of the visit was uneventful. When a guest (invited or self-invited) extends the invi-tation to more folks than the host is prepared for, the invitation protocol has been breeched.

Rosie said that she was somewhat sympathetic. When she was a young adult, she had barged in on a ninety-two year old aunt who lived in a small apartment in New York City. Rosie brought along her boyfriend as well as her girlfriend and the girlfriends boyfriend. Two young un-married couples must have been at once uncomfortable and offensive to this nonagenarian who managed to maintain her personal boundaries, dignity and self control and be a gracious hostess as well. She put the four-some up for the night, but insisted that the men sleep on the balcony and that they all leave the following morning.

Our glazier said that his son's friends visited. The two guys ate and drank everything and replenished nothing. Further, they scattered their belongings around the house. Although the guys wanted to extend the visit, the family said they couldn't accommodate them because they had other family obligations and drove them to the airport.

Ellen regularly hosts her nephew's friends from a nearby university. She is delighted to have the fun loving youthful company. Ellen has some strict rules, however.

Hookahs may be smoked only in the back yard. One morning she came down to find the tile on her kitchen counter had been scorched by someone who left his hookah next to the sink. As in this instance, Ellen's strategy for keeping her place clean is to dole out pails, sponges and cleaning supplies along with instructions for mopping up, cleaning up the bathrooms and kitchen so the house is always clean and tidy when she returns home from work.

In referring to the chapter on Invitations, perhaps even more care needs to be taken when extending hospitality to this particular group. It may be that our neurons in charge of social graces lie dormant until it is our turn to become hosts. So Beware!

-thirteen-

SUPER SENIOR CITIZENS
AS HOUSEGUESTS

"You are old, Father William," the young man said
"And your hair has become very white:
And yet you incessantly stand on you head —
Do you think, at your age, it is right?"

Lewis Carroll

In our age or perhaps all ages, it seems that we yearn to live forever and yet never grow old! That's a dream most of us share. And why not? During the past century the life expectancy in the U.S. has increased by some thirty years. Of course, much of this is due to a decline in infant mortality. However, better health care, diet, exercise, and increased income have brought a higher standard of living for most Americans. And this follows us into the retirement years. The designation, "Senior Citizen," probably emerged as a euphemism to avoid the label "elderly."

At what age do we acquire the "senior citizen" stamp? A clear time for affixing the label remains unclear. AARP letters arrive as we turn fifty when many of us feel that we have finally matured enough to have a genuine mid-life crisis or we are just deciding what we "really" want to do with the rest of our years. Grandma may have just treated herself to a new face-lift and her hair may be the latest shade of blonde while grandpa may be playing golf three day s a week and shooting in the 70's. Since most of us aren't ready to admit "elderly" applies to us — even unto the octogenarian years then exactly how do we define senior? This "down the road of life" label may well reflect one's own age. Anyone older than I am is my "senior."

Our seniors were brought up in their own distinct period of history and moved by different, food, music, manners, styles and political issues. Their own points of view were established when the world was a slightly different place. Because of better health care, food, exercise options, and stimulating intellectual opportunities, retirement age folks of sixty-five and more are living healthier and remaining mentally sharper than ever before.

Today many older adults may put off retirement or start a second career. Others take advantage of more stimulating intellectual and social life by moving to retirement communities where they can remain as active as they wish.

Another activity many seniors put off until they retire is travel. For seniors, travel is likely to mean a visit to see their children and grandchildren. That's right, more often than not; they are coming to see you!

When you plan activities for today's seniors, keep in mind that if they are in good health; they will most likely want to be included in all of your family's activities. And don't be surprised if they choose to play a starring role!

When we think about our senior house guests, the majority of the time we are talking about relatives. Close relatives that are parents and in-laws. One advantage to having parents visit is we know what to expect. Chances are you have visited them and they have been your guests many times before turning sixty-five. But seniors, including parents, have different needs from other guests. And you need to anticipate these needs as best you can and to make preparations accordingly.

As one's age advances, bodies begin to ache. Short-term memory is elusive, even if we prefer not to acknowledge it. However, as a retired English teacher, I'm here to let everyone know that there are a lot of sixteen year olds who can't remember to bring pencil, books, or homework to class and I've never heard even one plead he was experiencing a "senior moment."

Some problems may arise while entertaining senior citizens because they are often one's parents or in-laws. The difficulties that arise may have as much to do with the family relationship as with age. They are a generation or so in advance and fail to realize that they are no longer the parent in charge. The resulting friction may create confusion and hurt for both the host and their elders. I remember my own injured feelings when Mom came to visit and instead of approving my happy family, my home and my cooking, she straightened the pictures around the house (She never seemed to notice when the pictures in her house were cockeyed.) and ignored the inviting household comforts I had worked so hard to put together.

When a more disruptive parent or in-law, as houseguest, attempts to drive a wedge between family members, it is time to protect the needs of the primary family and invite the disrupter to leave.

Karen and Joe Smith, a young couple, live in Chicago; his family lives in Florida. After the birth of their first child, Joe's mother came to "help out" for a couple of weeks. She stayed for three months and proved to be the quintessential "mother-in-law-from hell." Her overbearing "know it all" attitude and disparaging remarks to her daughter-in-law upset the young couple. When their second child arrived, Joe told his mother that she could come and see the new baby, but she would have to stay in a hotel and stop criticizing his wife.

This is a great example of "take charge and protect the family" — even from one's own mother's behavior.

This is also a good time to point out that when a parent or in-law arrives to help out with a newborn that she or he should do just that —help. Babies are demanding and new moms are fragile; they need lots of rest. Though they need and probably are grateful for help around the house and with any other small children, the new mother is in no condition to entertain anyone. It is a wise elder guest who will ask the new mother just what she wants done around the house. Helping with meals, laundry, vacuuming, and dusting, along with small amounts of social-izing will go far to cement family relations. For purposes of bonding, the care of the infant should be left to the new mother. The wise guest will, sometime during each afternoon, announce that she is off to her room to read for a couple of hours and provide the new parent her own space and time for relaxing.

My own mother-in-law appeared a month after the birth of my first child. She was very disruptive, telling me not to rock the baby and became hostile when I ignored her advice. She came, prepared to stay for an undetermined length of time and I finally had to tell my husband to get her out, or I would leave. He finally, had to tell her to go home.

A parent may also have a habit that the next generation finds intolerable. Jimmy bluntly told his father, an alcoholic, that he would not be allowed to drink at his house. The father, desperate to visit his grand children, did, in fact, give up drinking for the duration of his visits with his son's family.

And Then There's The Kitchen:

    One night during a mother-in-law visit, Ginger put dinner in the oven and then went off to take a shower. When Ginger emerged from the bathroom, she smelled burning food. The mother —in-law was standing next to the stove in the kitchen and Ginger asked her why in the world she didn't turn off the oven and remove the food? The mother-in-law's sarcastic reply was, "I thought maybe you wanted it burned." Ginger and her husband decided, "No more house guests." Ginger apparently interpreted the mother- in-law's behavior as helpless and hopeless. To be fair to the mother-in-law who comes across as a bit daft, some folks are fussy about their kitchens and some guests are timid about overstepping boundaries.

    In spite of their resolve, Ginger's in-laws called a year later to announce (uninvited) that they would be coming back for a nine day stay. They understood that they would be staying in a motel. To help with the strain of expenses, the young couple lent the elder couple one of their three cars so they could sight —see and shop while the hosts were working. They were given Ginger's car, while Ginger drove the old beat-up vehicle to work. The seniors ate breakfast at the motel each morning, walked the beach and then returned to Ginger and Robert's house and simply sat there waiting for their hosts to return home and cook the evening meal for them. Ginger was infuriated. In addition, her mother-in-law has dietary issues and the older couple explained that it was too expensive to eat out. Ginger was gasping for patience when she relayed her irritation and hostage dilemma to me. Exasperated, she remarked, "We have only five days left before they leave!"

These in-laws left with the intention of traveling to the home of another son for an additional nine day visit.

When Celeste's mother-in-law came for a visit from Mexico, she refused to open a cupboard or touch anything in the kitchen. She apparently viewed her own kitchen as the place where she reined as queen and didn't want to step into her daughter-in-law's domain. This, of course, drove Celeste nuts since she didn't want to have to attend to every cup of coffee, glass of water etc. for an extended stay.

Judy was infuriated when she told her story about being held hostess hostage to her mother-in-law:

The woman, who never smiles, announced that she was coming to Carlsbad, CA from Mexico City to visit for a week. She knew full well that her grandson's Bar Mitzvah was scheduled two weeks after her departure date. Once ensconced in Judy's house, the mother-in-law began communicating with relatives in Mexico and it became obvious to Judy that she decided to stay the full three weeks rather than fly back and forth.

Judy was livid. She was quite certain that this dowager had manipulated her lengthy stay before she ever left home.

There are elders who reach an age where they may become either physically disabled or mentally befuddled. Dealing with houseguests who are in less than optimal health is apt to be an exasperating experience.

Sarah and Pauline are married to brothers. Their parents-in laws are both infirm and have special needs.

Gramps has asthma, has gone through two hip replacements and is nearly blind with macular degeneration; Gram has dementia. Because they are so debilitated, they rotate between their son's homes at opposite ends of the country and stay with each anywhere from ten days to three weeks at a time. Of course, it falls on the daughters-in-law to look after them. A loving sense of humor along with extreme patience helps these women manage through each visit.

These daughters-in-law are obviously both in love with their husbands and understand and appreciate the failing health of these elderly in-laws. They are clearly stumped and worried by the developing health problems and in a quandary about continuing to have them as house guests. These sisters-in-law do have each other so they can vent their frustrations with another understanding soul.

Abdul' hadn't seen his mother in six years, so he went to Somalia and brought her back to his home in Encinitas, CA. His wife, Allia, who has her own busy life assisting teenage Somalian girls gain an education in the U.S., found herself in charge of the mother-in-law she had never met.

This elderly woman who has encroaching dementia is beyond confusion in a strange culture. She often thinks Allia is the maid and has developed the habit of flinging Allia's 's bedroom door open in the morning, demanding that she get up and cook breakfast. Allia is in full charge of Abdul's mother all day every day. If Abdul or one of his brother's appears, Allia takes the opportunity to escape for an hour or so.

Allia emphasizes that Abdul is such a great guy that she is willing to continue with this program for awhile. They are sending the mother-in-law off to a brother's home in Minnesota for three weeks over the winter holidays while Allia and Abdul will visit her sister in New York.

Teresa, whose marvelous mother-in-law has a special reputation as a Houseguest from Heaven is continually frustrated by the less than heavenly behavior of her father-in-law.

> *If I had to find a problem with Grandma Joan staying with us for three months, it's that she doesn't come alone; she brings Grandpa. Grandpa's main job is to let Grandma wait on him hand and foot. I try to not let it irritate me, but one morning after Grandma Joan finally sat down to her breakfast and coffee, Grandpa looked at her plate and said, "Toast looks good, I'd like some toast," Grandma, of course got up to make him toast. I sternly said to Grandma, "Sit," and to Grandpa, "Make your own toast." Imagine the horror in my husband and mother-in-law's faces as I actually told Grandpa what to do!*

If a person appears to be particularly forgetful, sometimes gets lost in areas that ordinarily are familiar, and repeats the same question and doesn't remember the answer, s/he may be manifesting signs of developing dementia or Alzheimer's. Do attempt to be patient and kind. You could be next. The newspaper may be read over and over with each reading representing a new experience. Include these folks in the conversation and as many family activities as possible. They are still with you and need loving attention. This is your opportunity to be sensitive and learn about the feelings of those who are becoming disabled.

Though most senior citizens are perfectly capable of managing things for themselves, there may be some areas that need special consideration. Everyone, including hosts, needs some space and quiet time during any visit. Seniors usually need more rest than the younger generation. By all means, consider suggesting that it is fine to take a nap. The host might say, "I'm going to read a book for a couple of hours, you might like to nap." Because a strange household might be intimidating to members of an older generation, notes on how to use the microwave, toaster oven, washer, dryer, or other appliances might be helpful.

It is always necessary to be particularly aware of safety needs of seniors in the bedroom and bathroom. Along with nightlights, additional aids for seniors or others in the home with signs of failing health in guest bedrooms should include:

1. A flashlight and perhaps a bell or cell phone on the night stand. Waking alone, in pain or confusion in a strange place might be frightening to a senior guest. These inexpensive small tools can be used to alert others to "middle of the night" difficulties, help allay fears and make both guest and host feel more secure.

2. A fan might assist in air circulation during hot summer months. Some folks (both young and old) are lulled to sleep with the "white noise."

3. Plenty of clean linens, pillows and extra blankets or quilts.

4. A plastic non-absorbent mattress pad on the bed. This is desirable — even necessary — if there is any inkling that your senior guest may have incontinence problems.

5. A small basket with bottled water, power bars, and a few pieces of fruit, and wrapped cheese, crackers or candy—to help ward off middle of the night hunger pangs.

6. A few magazines or large print novels —appropriate for your particular senior would be a thoughtful gesture.

7. Be sure there is a rubber mat in the bottom of the tub or shower and a grab bare on the wall of the tub or shower.

8. Plastic or paper cups in the guest bathroom

9. Extra toothbrushes, toothpaste and mouthwash

10. Soft towels, shampoos, conditioner and soap are a must.

Slippery scatter rugs are also particularly hazardous when less sure footed elderly people are being hosted. Slipping, sliding and tripping are serious problems as we age.

Wheelchair ramps cost about $600.00 which is a bit steep for a lot of folks who entertain seniors in wheelchairs. Marty took care of the wheel chair ramp needs of his father-in-law by going to Home Depot and finding a great guy who made the right cuts in a piece of plywood for creating an inexpensive $40.00 ramp. This changed the life of the incapacitated senior. He is now able to easily roll out to the backyard on his own for family barbecues or reading in the sunshine.

My friend, Al, works out regularly at the YMCA is one of those seniors whose living history may enrich our lives during a houseguest visit. We need to be aware of some of the pain we cause them when they are ignored or even abused while visiting.

"*I was born in 1923. Those of you of my generation who read this will understand what I am saying and the younger generation will be astonished about what us old folks had to deal with in our youthful days.*

We lived our youthful days during the Depression Era when some families consisted of Ma and Pa and ten to fourteen children struggled for existence. Our house had two bedrooms and one bathroom, an attic and base-ment. Most of the attic was used as a bedroom – dorm style. The basement was home of the furnace, washing machine and storage bins for jars of vegetables and fruits that Mom canned when they were in season. Food was stored and used from season to season as few people had refrigerators in those days. There were eight of us chil-dren plus Ma and Pa. I had five sisters and two brothers. I was the seventh kid who wore hand-me-downs, home-made shirts, pants (knickers) and one sailor suit made by Mom. All Moms were great cooks, bakers and seam-stresses. When we were young and our families got together, our guests usually brought the children along. We kids would sit at a separate table; the parents and older kids, aunts and uncles sat at the big table. In those days, everyone brought food and there was always plenty to eat: homemade pies, cheesecake, ice cream, and root beer. Yummy yum yum. My taste buds still remember!

We didn't have much; we made our own recreation. Most of us were in the same situation. We all played with homemade games and played on the streets. There wasn't much traffic, because not many could afford cars. We were lucky in our youth.

I went to war in 1943. Luck was with me and I came home in 1945. My war was in Europe; I was a waist gunner on a B-24 Bomber. I had many close calls, but the Good Lord took care of me and I came home safe and sound.

Now at eighty-three, my left leg from below the knee is gone. It was amputated when I was seventy-four years old. In my youth I called people who wore glasses, four eyes; adults who lost a limb were called peg leg; retarded children were ignored and scorned.

I was one of those obnoxious kids. During the 20's and 30's we didn't know any better. Today's children are not showing respect for their elders and the disabled either. Camaraderie among them is almost non-existent. I can say this because I am now the recipient of this derision and scorn. My granddaughter is eighteen and she ignores me because I am handicapped. I can see the repulsion and embarrassment in her face. I blame her parents, and I know there are many parents who do not teach their children that humans at whatever age and in whatever condition want and need to be a part of the family group. I am a member of the Greatest Generation who deserves better. I will survive this pain. The children are the losers."

Senior citizens are our living history. Instead of being irritated or bored by the same old stories, get out a tape recorder, or better yet, a camcorder; interview this family gem and get the family history for your personal archives. The older generation will surely feel honored and someday, the kids will be grateful

-fourteen-

CANINE, FELINE AND
FEATHERED GUESTS

"The best thing about animals is that they don't talk much"

Thornton Wilder

Never mind that Kristie's former schoolmate arrived for an overly long five week visit; she brought along her tiny dog that Kristie dubbed the Little Black Poop Ball. Yup, this adorable black teacup poodle pooped everywhere around the house when it wasn't getting lost in the neighborhood. Several times Kristie took it upon herself to go in search of Poop Ball when her laid-back guest said, "Oh he'll find his way back."

Another pet story:

Beth related that she had expected to entertain her friend Ramona and her three children. However she wasn't, prepared for the uninvited beagle that promptly marked his territory in every corner of her house.

It may be difficult for a guest who travels with his pets to understand, but not everyone is going to love and appreciate his dog, cat, hamster, parrot, lizard, or tortoise as he does. The truth is, most of us love to pamper our own pets, but we don't want other people's pets in our home and that is why an invitation to a houseguest rarely includes them. To expect a host to lodge pets is beyond audacious.

Animals, like all living things on the planet, have their own individual personalities and characters. Some animals are wonderful travelers and visitors; others are best left at home or in a kennel. More often than not, potential hosts are less than thrilled to have an animal as a guest.

The issues of extending invitations to pets — or not—is dealt with in the chapter on "Invitations." It is completely inconsiderate for a guest to appear with their animal in tow, believing that others will be as enamored of this creature as they. Horror stories of animal guests abound and every host is within his rights to resist entertaining animals. It is not unknown for a nervous animal that is out of his own territory to become sick and vomit or even develop a case of diarrhea.

I fully understand the guest who has an animal that he can't bear to leave at home alone. My Petite Shetland Sheep Dog, Foxy, is very social, docile and sweet. She hates being left at home alone. I take her with me even when she has to wait for a couple of hours in the car (windows rolled down some for ventilation and a glass of water to slake her thirst). Once I made the mistake of asking a friend if we could bring Foxy along for her dinner party. The hostess was close to apoplectic, fearing that Foxy would pee on her oriental carpets. Foxy would burst before she would have an accident, but I was wrong to attempt to wrangle an invitation for my pet.

In the long ago, a wonderful family friend, who could well have afforded hotel accommodations, came across the country to visit us with her new husband and her aged Chihuahua. The dog was incontinent, but, nevertheless, she slept with the dog in our guest bed. One morning she came out to embrace me and I involuntarily gagged. I'm certain she had no idea that she smelled like her decrepit pet. This story reminds me of Candy, a character, in Steinbeck's Of Mice and Men. *Candy's ageing stinking sick old dog was the only object of love for this poor old man to cling to in his lonely transient life.*

I was thirty years old when I entertained this dear woman; I had no experience with this sort of dilemma. If I encountered this sort of problem today, I might enthuse over her sweet pet and then tell her I would "let" her make a bed for him in the garage.

Louise and Harry received a call from Harry's cousin whom they hadn't seen in twenty years. The cousin said he and his family were visiting the area and wanted to stop by to say, "Hello." Sure, why not meet up again with these cousins/strangers.

The family arrived with their baby and dog. The cousin then asked if they knew of a nearby hotel where they could stay. Since Louise and Harry also had a baby, they invited the family to spend the night at their home. The folks were fine, but the dog was crazed! He ran non-stop round and round the house. At bedtime, they put a gate up at the kitchen door. During the night, the dog scratched up the kitchen cabinets and finally bounded over the kitchen gate to spend the night in the room with his owners.

This ranks as a visiting pet horror story. Surely the cousin knew that his dog was a problem. To have accepted an overnight invitation was thoughtless and rude beyond belief. The cousin was responsible for repairing the damage to the cabinets, though I'd be willing to bet that there was no offer to make amends.

People traveling with their pets should understand and undertake full responsibility for their animals.

Carl and Kari have four beautiful special breed dogs that travel with them most everywhere. The dogs are trained to stay in kennels if necessary. When they travel to visit friends around the country with their dogs are usually welcomed because they take total care of the animals. Carl and Kari do all of the feeding, walking and caring for these special canine visitors who are a pleasure to have as guests.

George, the plumber, who moved to San Diego from Texas, had to deal with his uninvited long term interloper acquaintances and their dog.

He would come home after a long day at work, kick off his shoes and find himself treading in wet spots on the carpet and discovering dog dirt behind the television set. This gentle former gang member with tattoos up both arms, put up with these freeloaders along with dog piss and poop until his month to month long lease on the furnished apartment was up and he moved out – leaving the interlopers to their own dirty devices.

Nancy invited her sister for a visit. The sister refused to travel without her dog. Finally, a less than enthusiastic Nancy reluctantly agreed to let the dog come along, but established some rules which pretty much kept the dog quartered outside on the patio.

During the time my daughter, Diane, was in college and living in her make-shift shanty with her beloved cat, a former high school classmate showed up –an interloper with two German Sheppard dogs. This arrangement lasted a couple of weeks until, Diane, fed up, told this thoughtless clueless over-stepper that she and her dogs had to be gone by the time she returned from work that day. They vanished, but the miserable memory lingers on.

For many of us, our animals are, indeed, the objects of our affection. "Love me, love my dog/cat/pet" is a cliché that doesn't always resonate with our friends and acquaintances. More often than not, it is outside the tolerance of those who entertain house guests.

Jean was temporarily out of a place to live. She called Barbara and said, "I know you will let me stay with you until my house is available." Barbara agreed that Jean could spend a month with her, but she specifically told her that she would not be allowed to bring her pets along. While Barbara was out of the house, Jean smuggled in her dog and parrot and stashed them in the bedroom closet. Barbara came in one day and told Jean that she could smell the dog. Jean lied, "Oh no, I don't have the dog." For some unfathomable reason, at that moment—Barbara slid open the closet door; the parrot squawked and the dog popped out revealing the deception. Barbara, in no uncertain terms told this refugee that she had to move out—immediately.

Joan and John often host Mary and Joe who refuse to travel or visit without their beloved cat. Joan invites them to stay, but the cat has his own quarters – in the garage. Joan and John have beautiful furniture that they don't want shredded by their friend's pet. This arrangement seems to work for everyone – including the cat.

Another instance of animal intrusion was related by Hannah.

> *Her son lives in San Francisco and visits her home in Cardiff, CA. once a year. He brings along his two dogs, a rabbit and a gecko. Hannah's cat is bent on attacking the rabbit (busy pooping in its cage in a small bathroom) and would relish the gecko for a quick lunch.*

Hannah's situation resembles an old Tom and Jerry cartoon, but she puts up with the unusual menagerie in order to have her son with her for a short time. Mayhem is another word for the misery inflicted on the household with these uninvited visitors from the animal kingdom.

As related in another chapter, I had house guests who showed up with a parrot and six tortoises. Since I didn't expect any animals and my condominium complex had a "no pet" policy, I was very irritated at this audacious unexpected inclusion and intrusion and let my overstepping guests know that they had to pack up their animals and leave.

If you have agreed to allow a guest to bring along his pet, then it is the responsibility of the guest to care for the animal in every way. He needs to bring along his pet's food and provide it for the duration of the visit. He should also bring a bed for the animal. The guest/pet owner also needs to make sure the animal has plenty of water and is exercised several times daily. It is also the responsibility of the guest to clean up any messes that the pet might deposit in the house or in the yard and pay for anything that is damaged or broken by the pet.

As a host who has included animals on her guest list, I have provided the pets with couple of inexpensive toys (Our dog loves to play tug of war). Even some doggie or cat treats would be a nice courtesy. Our dog also loves those teeth cleaning "green bones." The dog needs to be monitored, though, to be sure it isn't ingesting too much at one time.

If animals are members of the host's home, it may be necessary to separate his meal from others so there is no snapping or snarling.

> *Joy and her husband had a cat and a dog and both animals had free run of their small hotel on a lake in Arkansas. Joy put the Meow Mix on a table in the reception area so the dog couldn't get to it. One of the guests commented that her colorful little snacks were delicious!*

If there is any reason that a host family is reluctant to have an animal in or around his home, then it is necessary for the invited guest to make other arrangements for the animal and possibly himself. We all need to keep in mind that not everyone is an animal lover and many homes don't function as an animal kennel. Pet sitting businesses abound in almost every community. If the neighbors won't volunteer to take care of the animals while you are out of town, call a reputable pet sitter. You and your pets will have a comfortable safe vacation away from one another and the host will be grateful for your forethought.

-fifteen-

THE GATHERING FAMILY STORM

"Molly, my sister, and I fell out,
And what do you think it was all about?
She loved coffee and I loved tea,
And that was the reason we couldn't agree."

Marguerite deAngeli's
Book of Nursery And Mother Goose Rhymes

It usually seems like a grand idea to get the family all together for a great holiday celebration or vacation. Each household throughout the country looks forward to celebrating the holidays with family. We are impacted by the "Happy Holiday" marketing blitz and Norman Rockwell's Thanksgiving treasure. The illustration features a glowing family gathering with grandma and grandpa, grown children and all the grandchildren happily salivating over a turkey at on the holiday table.

An hour after everyone has unpacked and settled in, the fantasy of the joyful family reunion begins to fade. Reality arrives with relatives who, more often than not, may fail to observe the host family routine. Grandpa usurps the TV remote, the kids go into over-drive, Aunt Tillie stuffs the refrigerator and cupboards with her own foods and Grandma launches into a kitchen takeover.

ENTERTAINING FAMILY MEMBERS HAS TO BE ONE OF THE MOST EXPLOSIVE ISSUES ON THE PLANET.

There are examples of family difficulties throughout this guide that may occur during a visit and it is almost impossible to begin to discuss all the relatives, their affiliations and the issues that might arise. Often relationships within families are tangled webs with mom and pop issues along with sibling rivalries going back to childhood. Most families have, accumulated baggage that is often carried right along for the holiday visit. For some folks, inviting family for a holiday celebration turns the household into a war zone. Old irritations that have lurched into resentments and finally morphed into grudges solidly cast in stone may become toxic conversational crosscurrents, or at the slightest provocation, noisy arguments. For most of us, thoughtful pre-planned entertainment is a must if we want the visit to be pleasant rather than a battleground.

As with any other invitation, the host and hostess are in charge of the visit no matter what the other family relationships might be. They create the invitation, make the sleeping arrangements, plan menus and establish the entertainment schedule. The host's position in the family hierarchy doesn't matter; the host and hostess are in charge and call the shots.

Rita and Jay live in Walnut Creek, CA.; they each come from a large family of parents and siblings. Everyone gets along beautifully, except for Jay's brother, Jeremy, who seems to be narcissistic, and his wife, Joyce, who decided that she was in competition with Rita. Since Jeremy and Joyce live in Grosse Pointe, Michigan, the family encounters are infrequent.

One November Joyce called Rita to ask what they were doing over Christmas. Rita thought Joyce was calling to invite them for the holidays; she told her that her parents would be spending Christmas with them and that they would be at home. Joyce was calling to wrangle an invitation for her family of six. Rita told her that they would help find them a hotel, but Joyce balked. She said, "We want to come to California for the holidays and we need to stay with you because we can't afford a hotel." Fueled by a need to maintain a semblance of family harmony, Rita asked her parents to visit another time and then agreed to entertain this aggressive sister-in-law and her brood. The holidays went downhill from there. Rita had to relegate her eldest daughter to a walk-in closet for a bedroom.

Joyce's boys were undisciplined. One evening they removed the pepperoni from a pizza and threw the pieces around the kitchen. Joyce and Jeremy were almost no help with the chores and they did not help buy food or take the host family out to dinner. Rita spent an inordinate amount of time avoiding the family storm; she cloistered herself in her own bedroom until the visit was over.

I later called Rita to ask what she would do differently if she were asked to repeat that particular Christmas scenario. She then told me that Joyce had also invited her mother-n-law, who was Rita's husband's mother, to join them on the trip. Because she loved her mother-in-law (since deceased) and wanted her to be happy, the situation would have to be played out the same way. She did say that if Joyce were to call now and ask to visit that she would simply lie and tell her that they wouldn't be home.

Often there is an assumed designated entertainer/host family for major holiday events. When this tacitly appointed individual rebels, and declines to host holiday events, the other relatives have difficulty understanding why he is reluctant to continue in this good old familiar mode. After many years of doing doormat duty, enough becomes enough.

For many years from December 23rd until New Years day, grandparents Maria and Jaime hosted their large brood of six, along with their spouses, children, and step-children for the Christmas holiday season. Old-age was creeping up on them and they finally told everyone they were finished doing the honors. It came as an uncomfortable shock for the fun loving siblings and their families that mom and pop would deprive them of this seasonal custom.

Too much of a good thing can become tedious. Rotation of the week long holiday hospitality was in order. It isn't surprising that no other freeloading family members were willing to open their home to maintain the holiday celebration.

Nancy and Ralph, who had become the chronic ritual hosts for all of her large family's holiday gatherings, finally simply stepped back. She made other plans for her own husband and children during that time. They excluded brothers, sisters, in-laws, nieces, nephews and even the family matriarch and patriarch. They chose quiet close family togetherness rather than the expected noisy expensive work-laden holiday celebration that everyone had come to expect. After a couple of years, it became obvious that this couple had ended their tour as annual hosts. Although they occasionally entertained family members – one small family at a time; the big holiday gatherings were lost and gone forever – buried in the past along with Nancy and Ralph's irritated feelings of being used and abused.

Nancy later reported that while no other family member has offered to step up to the plate and entertain for the holidays; there has been something of a transformation of attitude among parents and siblings. Many of these relatives now invite Nancy and Ralph for dinners at nice restaurants or other social outings that were missing from the yearly agenda before they rejected their role as accommodating doormats.

By rejecting their co-dependent behavior, they are enjoying their own newly discovered self-esteem, independence and respect.

On the other side of the holiday entertaining coin is the person who holds the rest of the family hostage by controlling every holiday and insisting all celebrations be held at his/her house.

Rachel was fuming! She shared that she was upset and disappointed because hosting the big Chanukah celebration at her house had become tradition. A pushy sister-in-law decided that she was going to have the next family celebration at her house; Rachel definitely felt her family tradition was being usurped and her hospitality truncated.

This may become a serious family problem, especially when others would like to display their entertaining skills. It may be best to just say, "Our immediate family has decided to celebrate the holiday in our own home, if you would like to join us, we would love to have you." No excuses are necessary for making your own plans for your own family. If someone wants to pout, or worse, have a temper tantrum; it's their upset. Ignore it and go on with your own plans.

The following story was written especially for this section by a disgruntled sister-in-law. Her views and opinions might be shared by many who are expected to entertain thoughtless family members.

In 2005, we were so fortunate (tongue in cheek) to share our home with my brother-in-law, my husband's brother. It happened to be more time than we have spent with him during the last twenty years.

His arrival for our daughter's graduation in May began inauspiciously. He had rented a car upon his arrival in Los Angeles and as he entered the freeway ramp, he rear-ended the car stopped in front of him. You could read the other car's license plate # on the front of the rental. This incident, of course colored his whole visit. He spent this special occasion ruminating about a car!

We had a new house and we had put in white carpet. I mention this because I served him a Diet Pepsi that he promptly spilled, leaving a large pool on the living room carpet. Certainly, there was no effort on his part to help clean up the mess and there was no remorse. And this was just the beginning! Our T.V room doubles as a guest room with a new love seat that is also a single sofa sleeper.

The first morning after his arrival, and an evening of drinking, I came downstairs to feed my cats. I found no one in the bed, the mattress on the porch and the sheet wadded up in a ball in the yard. My brother-in-law was asleep on the living room couch. I could only surmise what may have happened. My worst fears were confirmed. He had soiled the sleeper. His liquid consumption the night before had taken its toll!

During the graduation party, my husband's brother fell asleep on the couch, an unwelcome decoration, and never met any of my daughter's guests

The final night of the visit, the brother-in-law again drank too much, started an argument and then abruptly packed and left.

Part of my upset is: Where was my husband during all of this? What was he doing? Has he no respect and pride in our house? Are his loyalties so misguided that he allowed an intruder in our home to treat it with less respect than a Motel 6?

Just because it's family, do you have to put up with a rude slob?

It is best if everyone can manage to remember that just because you're family doesn't make it all right to barge in without invitation or notice. The host family plans ahead, hoping to avoid unpleasant surprises.

One Christmas Helen invited her parents who lived in Michigan to share Christmas with her family in Florida.

She thought it would be an opportunity for her three children ages nine, eleven and thirteen to have some time with Grandma and Grandpa and develop a closer family relationship. She spent a great deal of time planning menus and events for a happy holiday. Grandma and Grandpa happily arrived—with her brother, his wife from Indiana and their three small boys in tow! She was certain her mother was envisioning a happy holiday surrounded by all of her grandchildren. Unfortunately, Helen was in shock. She hadn't invited these extra five people, hadn't planned for gifts for the toddlers nor had she planned on feeding, rooming, and entertaining these extra people. Bah! Humbug! Helen was livid! Her brother's family had a reputation for never having their own "at home" family Christmas. They always took their kids either to her family in Argentina or to Helen's parent's home in Michigan. Helen's dream plans for having her kids spend time alone with their grandparents were dashed. Was she selfish? You bet! Her mood must have been obvious because the extra family left on December 23rd. That was many years ago, but Helen insists that she didn't and doesn't feel guilty. Just because they were family didn't entitle them to alter her Christmas plans.

Often, it isn't just a holiday that draws family together, but frequently there is the built-in belief that family should have an open door policy no matter the time of year and no matter that the intended hosts may have other plans or prefer their privacy. Whether the setting is urban or country, whether the target hosts are close or distant relatives, often the attitude is, "We are family, so naturally, we are always welcome." Family members are expected to rally 'round and provide accommodations and food even if the family members haven't been invited. It may come as a nasty shock to some, but very often this entitlement view is out of whack with current lifestyles in the U.S.

All too often family members — running the gambit from very close to shoestring—somehow imagine that blood or marriage ties entitle them to a place at the fireside of a relative any old time they feel like it. Then the lucky designated host/entertainer is expected to do his best to accommodate and please the "family." The "good ole days" of expecting entitlement lodging and/or hospitality is long gone — or should be. You, as family hosts, should expect to be treated with the same consideration that would be extended to "outsiders." The assumption that there is an ongoing "open season" for your relatives to avail themselves of your hospitality or guest quarters is a false premise. Because you continue to play the role of doormat and allow them to take advantage, they may conclude that you are "happy" to accommodate and even underwrite their vacation year after year.

> *Samantha shared that her nephew, who lives close by, called one morning to say that his parents were visiting from another state and they would like to get together that day. Samantha hadn't seen her brother and his wife in several years and supposed that she and her husband were being invited to the nephew's home. Well, uh, . . .no! They thought they would come to Samantha's. She explained that they had other plans that day and she wouldn't be able to fix dinner, but if they wanted to drop by for a drink at about seven in the evening that would be fine. They came, they drank, they ate (all of the snacks from the pantry and two refrigerators) and stayed until at about 11:00 p,m. Her husband finally said something nice about a politician detested by her brother and they immediately left. (With no thanks.)*

Dianne has a note on the door of her quilting room which reads:

"Friends welcome,

Family needs an invitation."

Denise who lives in Phoenix, Arizona, developed a pattern of avoiding the unbearably warm summer weather by assuming that her brother's guest house in Santa Cruz, CA was at her family's disposal each year. Even though separate quarters were available, they were invading privacy and territory. Denise's brother and his wife are resentful, but they are reluctant to in any way reveal their true feelings because Denise is a family member. Once the hostess did tell her that they couldn't invite them because they would be out of town at the time of the planned visit. Denise persevered, saying that they could manage without the host family being present. In true Doormat fashion, the target hosts relented.

This woman harbors a sense of entitlement that overwhelms the atmosphere and ambience of the host family. Denise's motives for encroaching on the privacy of her brother and his family probably were multifaceted. The issues of climate and economics must have been uppermost on her list of reasons for taking her yearly vacation in her brother's guest house. It was certainly a considerable saving on her yearly vacation budget. Denise probably harbors the attitude of, "We're no trouble." The brother and his wife are perhaps fearful of rupturing family ties. The doormat syndrome continues uninterrupted, but the built-up resentment is apt to explode in another way at another time, and everyone will wonder why.

Communication is the key here. The next time the sister-in-law calls, she needs to be told that the guest house is closed for the summer or that they no longer entertain. It's fine to say, "We are in social overload and need our privacy. If you are coming to Long Beach, let us know where you are staying and perhaps we could meet somewhere for lunch."

The lovely Mexican hospitable phrase, "Mi casa es su casa" may on occasion boomerang.

Marta and Isael work long hours in their coffee/ snack shop in Poway, Ca. Isael's cousin, Eduardo, works nearby in construction, commuting from his home in Tijuana. One day when the traffic delay was extraordinary, he asked Isael if he could spend the night instead of returning to Tijuana. One overnight led to another and another — and — another! Soon, Eduardo was spending the week days with Isael and Marta, going home only on weekends.

This hard working couple lost their privacy to a freeloading family member who took the Mexican phrase literally. Mexican culture probably precludes letting the overstepping family member know that the situation was uncomfortable and awkward. In cases like this, the couple might have made plans for their own vacation and then told the cousin that he wouldn't be able to stay in the house while they were away. Upon their return, they could change the locks and refuse him entry — or simply tell him that things have changed and they can't have him as a visitor.

One family in a southern state escapes the long hot summer by moving in on an ageing aunt who lives in a large farm house in northern Maine. The kids get to tramp the woods, do a little fishing, and spot some wild life now and then as well as pitch a little dung from the barn to prove they are there to help. The aunt provides the accommodations – gratis. Nice deal, huh? This nephew is an executive with a large company and can well afford to entertain his family in luxury. In spite of his upscale salary, his motive appears to be, in part, saving money. He also has a large ego, so his presence is often viewed by the farm relatives as grand-standing his superior lifestyle. Since there is a lake nearby with cottages that could be rented very reasonably, the aunt needs to tell this interloper and his tribe that having house guests is too much for her. She could then arrange for him to rent a cottage on the lake and visit her when the family gathers for special summer picnics.

Claire has her own continuing horror story about family wranglers and she doesn't seem to know how to deal with the issue.

Her husband, Marvin, has a nephew who calls two or three times a year and asks if it's okay for his family to visit. Marvin always says, "Sure." Then when these folks appear, Marvin leaves town on business. Claire then finds herself stuck with these folks in the house with an open ended visit.

If I were Claire, I might consider undermining the next visit with some well thought out passive aggressive moves, making it so uncomfortable that they would plan for an early departure. Some suggestions: empty the swimming pool, empty all kitchen cupboards and the refrigerator of food, clear the bathroom cabinets of soap and toilet paper, give the cleaning lady a three week vacation and have the gardener dump a load of fresh manure on the front lawn. But why punish yourself? A better solution would be to have a serious discussion with Marvin. She should insist that he either invite his nephew when he will be home to entertain this relative himself or find the nephew and his family other accommodations

Darcy contradicts herself when she maintains that she has never had a bad houseguest experience because then she goes on to say that after a few days, she begins to feel herself becoming irritated over petty issues such as clutter, stacks of laundry, scattered dirty dishes and a disorganized refrigerator. Her formula involves limiting family visits to five days. Her teenage girls are welcome to bring their friends home for a visit any time — just keep the five-day boundary intact.

Most of us want to do the "right" thing by our family members, and extending our hospitality on occasion is one of those "right" things.

Kathy and Nick invited Kathy's folks out to California to escape the miserable winter in Massachusetts. Kathy and Nick have four children, but they gave up their own master bedroom so the visiting parents would have a nice place to sleep. They also let the parents use their car. (Kathy's dad had hip problems and sleeping on a futon wouldn't have worked for him). Mom and Pop stayed for seven weeks. While the social benefits included sharing morning coffee, newspapers and conversation, the drawbacks became uncomfortable for both couples. Giving up the master bedroom certainly seemed like the good thing to do, but these young parents lost an important private territory. Time, space and privacy probably became issues for everyone. Kathy's mom said that it was a mistake to stay so long with her daughter's family. Subsequent visits by these parents are spent at a local hotel and they rent their own car.

Most of us envision a harmonious family gathering and may go out of our way to set aside the time to create the setting for that to happen. When our dreams go unrealized or the plans are high jacked or totally flop, we may have to accept the disappointment and try to understand that not every problem has a diplomatic solution.

> *One mother, anguished by the rift between her two daughters who lived many states apart, invited the family from far away to spend the weekend. Josephine, the older daughter, according to both her and her husband, was grieving over the loss of her sister's friendship. Pauline, the younger daughter, who lived within driving distance of the mother's house, agreed to appear (as a friendly surprise) for dinner during Josephine's visit. The idea was that they might begin the hatchet burying process. Unfortunately, when Pauline appeared, "grieving Josephine," rather than embracing her sister and perhaps letting her know how much she had missed the relationship, lashed out in a temper tantrum. She demanded to know why her sister hadn't spoken to her for so long. The unabated crying and pouting was upsetting to everyone present.*

> *The elder daughter charged that her mother was at fault by not letting her know that her sister would be present for dinner. The family has never recovered. Josephine is now totally out of touch with both Pauline and her mother.*

While the family dynamic was fragile before the attempt at resuming the sibling relationship, the lesson here is to avoid hidden agendas of amateur diplomacy. At best, the visit might have had a more comfortable resolution if both daughters had been apprised of the guest list.

It is possible for family members to become interlopers who imagine that bread and board are available any time they decide to show up on the doorstep. With "family" the boundaries tend to be fuzzier than those of friends and acquaintances. For some reason relatives have an attitude of "belonging" even if the house isn't theirs and never will be. The imagined happy family gathering may well become a houseguest nightmare.

EXAMPLE #1

Sheila and Dave, newlyweds, had just relocated to San Diego when Dave's mother came to visit. Her critical eye surveyed the new living quarters and she began suggesting all sorts of furnishings the couple needed to equip their new home – things the couple found unnecessary and couldn't afford. This controlling woman cast a disapproving eye on the draperies and took them down. She then took it upon herself to invite all of Dave's new colleagues for a dinner party at the couple's home, scheduling the event to begin long before Sheila could get home from the law office. Sheila blew! This lovely bright attorney confronted her mother-in-law with a verbal lashing that included a string of curses inconsistent with her normal demeanor. Although this happened many years ago; the mother-in-law and daughter-in-law remain estranged.

EXAMPLE #2

Bonnie and Ned were moving into a new apartment in a beach town close to San Diego when Bonnie's sister, Jerri, called to say that she was coming to visit for a month to escape the cold weather. They told her that she was arriving just as they were moving, so there was no place for her to stay. No problem, "How about my staying with Ned's parents in that big house high on the hill in Del Mar? Sure enough, she was comfy in the big house with near perfect strangers and stayed on for three weeks before Ned finally told her she had to leave. He bought a Greyhound bus ticket for her back to Mammoth.

A couple of years later this same sister once again announced that she was coming to visit. Bonnie and Ned, this time, set the limit of the visit to two weeks. Predictably, when the two weeks had elapsed, Jerri made no move to leave. Once again Ned played the role of bouncer. He told his sister-in-law that he was buying her airline ticket back to Mammoth. Jerri, a recovering alcoholic, pouted and announced that if this happened she would start drinking again. Determined not to be held hostage by these threats, Ned bought the ticket and put Jerri on the plane. True to her declared intent, Jerri started drinking on the plane and by the time she reached her destination, the airline was calling Bonnie and Ned to find out who she was and where she lived. It has been a few years since this incident, but Bonnie and Ned are still shaking their heads.

EXAMPLE #3

Dean is basically a vagrant who lives in the woods in a tent and travels with his belongings in a back pack. He was visiting San Diego because his favorite football team, The Raiders, was playing The Chargers in the Super Bowl and he just had to be here for that game. A week into the stay, the Raiders lost and Dean was so depressed that he just couldn't move out of the house. After two weeks, the couple had had it. Paul took Dean to a campsite on the beach at Carlsbad where Dean said he could spend the night for $5.00. Presumably Dean hitch-hiked back to his tent in the woods of northern California.

EXAMPLE #4

Jo Ann was a bride of nine months. She and her husband, a Navy pilot, lived in Texas. His twenty year old sister who lived in Montana decided she was going to bring a friend and come for a visit. After two weeks, the friend returned to Montana, but the sister, Gloria, stayed on — for two years.

Gloria found employment working in a drugstore; she created a social life with military personnel in the area; she worked, partied, played, paid no rent and did no housework. Some tensions did arise and Gloria said that she knew she should be paying rent, but that was never forthcoming. It wasn't until Jo Ann's second child was due that Gloria moved – without as much as a "thank you."

This young adult obviously felt entitled to move in with her brother and his wife because she was "family." The bride was too inexperienced to anticipate this long term event and both she and her husband felt too intimidated to establish any house rules even after the visit dragged on too long. It was, of course, the husband's responsibility to speak to his sister. But since he was often away on missions, he was less troubled than his bride by the long term intrusion. This is an example of a clear need for written boundaries. If there hadn't been two small children, the presence of this third party would have been more of a clear threat to the marriage.

Sharon and Doug Gallagher were leaving on a vacation to visit their daughter in Colorado. Sharon told her sister, Betty, that she and her husband were welcome to stay at their home in La Jolla while the Gallagher's were away. The Gallagher home is one of pristine elegance filled with beautiful antiques, and oriental rugs. When they returned home, Sharon was furious to learn from neighbors that Betty and her husband had not only brought their dog, but had also taken it upon themselves to invite their daughter and her husband along with their two rambunctious grandchildren, all of whom stayed at their house for a week.

Betty was secretive about inviting her daughter and her family to join her at the Gallagher's because she realized she was acting inappropriately. This can be prevented. Should you entrust your property to a relative, ask in advance about the number of guests. Follow it up in writing if you do not want them to have pets in your home or other guests unless cleared in advance with you.

A difficult experience with family interlopers occurred one summer when Sandra was working two jobs and going to school. Without first calling, her brother, his wife and three kids appeared, from the opposite coast and asked if they could take her out to dinner. Nice. Then, they decided that the sister-in law and the three boys would stay at Sandra's place for a week before meeting her brother in Las Vegas for a family vacation the following week. Sandra put aside some of the duties of her second job and played the proper hostess role by cooking for them and escorting them around town. Finally, they left on Thursday to finish their vacation in Las Vegas. Two days later as Sandra was preparing to attend class across town, the doorbell rang. It was the sister-in-law and the three boys — back. They had been waiting outside in a rented car since 5:00 a.m. The family had decided that they should return to Aunt Sandra's because her brother was going away on business. Their feeble excuse was — there was not enough for a young family to do in Las Vegas. While Sandra loved these people, her very full schedule made it beyond inconvenient to have visitors at her place any longer. She simply ignored them for the remainder of the week. Sandra suspected that their attitude was, "Gee, family is family" and it would never occur to them to call ahead and ask if a visit would be convenient.

For many, that which belongs to one family member belongs to all—for these there is no awareness that other family members may have developed their own lifestyle that doesn't include uninvited guests.

Family friction is apt to become more apparent when a new spouse moves into the old family quarters. Adult children who were brought up in the home may harbor a sense of ownership out of proportion to reality. During their visits, control issues may surface over the new family dynamics. Blended families more often than not encounter some snags while adjusting to new step-parents and stepchildren. If possible, it is always best for those in the re-marrying mode to seek out a new home that the new team owns jointly or is covered by a prenuptial agreement. This provides the newlyweds joint jurisdiction over the property while the "steps" are elevated to the status of cherished guests.

It was a second marriage for Shirley and Gene. Shirley moved into Gene's large home expecting to be in charge. It didn't happen. Gene's adult children still considered this their home and set about undermining any family dinners or holiday arrangements that Shirley planned. They still had their old stuffed animals living in the closets and Shirley didn't dare move them.

During family get-togethers, Gene's adult offspring took over the kitchen and set the agenda for the gatherings. Shirley's frustrations were so intense that she went to counseling for help. While matters have improved somewhat, tensions still exist and there is a deep scar on the marriage.

Most of us relish the idea of a happy harmonious family gathering. Blood is thicker than water and we savor the idea of sticking together in bonded family relationships. Family habits, customs, rituals, traditions, and ceremonies should have the capacity to bind us together. The mental picture of family members embracing one another, enthusing over how the kids have grown, reminiscing over food and drink after visiting local points of interest and creating a new page in the book of family memories may not come off as envisioned. Perhaps a vibrant pervasive sense of humor is a powerful tool for establishing accord. Sumptuous food, and a willingness for everyone to pitch in and help with the chores can go far to make the dream a reality. It's time for us as family hosts to step up, and exert our strength and to both maintain privacy and entertain family on our own terms.

RobSmaiL

-sixteen-

MUDDLING THROUGH MEALS

" 'Tis a privilege high to have dinner and tea
Along with the Red Queen, the White Queen and me!"

Queen Alice
Through the Looking Glass
Lewis Carroll

T he highlight of many visits is a meal – or the remembrance of a meal – whether it is a multi-course dinner in an exquisite restaurant or a picnic on the beach at sunset. As the hostess, you have the opportunity (or the duty) to "treat" guests to eating experiences. Whether it is the food itself, ("We've got a bushel of Maryland blue Crab!") or the preparation ("Jim's actually going to let you watch him prepare and smoke those North Carolina spare ribs.") or the conversation that ensues, meals with your chosen guests can be memorable.

And if your houseguests are with you for several days or weeks, you'll have the opportunity to create many memories. Houseguests do require nourishment – usually lots of it – beginning with breakfast, moving on to lunch, snacks, cocktail hour appetizers, dinner, and even midnight munchies. Just remember: the host's turf is the host's turf is the host's turf! Guests who don't understand this may overstep this boundary, and the results can have a deleterious effect on the visit.

Although Abigail had set the stage to entertain her husband's brother and his wife, Martha, a clash of wills initiated a kitchen skirmish on the first morning of the visit. Martha met Abigail in the kitchen and announced, much to the embarrassment of her husband, that she and Tom wanted sausage and waffles for breakfast. Smart Abigail, in her own resolute style, proclaimed the kitchen to be her domain and that her guests would eat what she prepared. Martha backed down, ate what she was served, and tempered her controlling attitude for the duration of the visit.

Of course, as the hostess, it is your duty to ascertain if there are any food issues before your guests arrive and then to make allowances for religious prohibitions and allergies. Beyond that, it is your privilege to plan the menus. If you want your guests to participate in menu planning and preparation, just ask!

Usually we will enjoy our visitors more if kitchen duties are minimal and fun. Even those of us who love to cook and feed people can get into trouble by trying to do too much with too little time and too many folks around. After all, lifestyles have changed considerably since the days when our mothers dominated the kitchen scene creating everything from scratch.

The faster paced life style most of us have adopted requires us to plan ahead when it comes to meal preparation. This is doubly true when guests are to be present. With the variety of foods available in specialty shops, big box stores, and the local supermarket, we can plan all our meals ahead of time and present a lovely table with nutritious, tasty food requiring a minimum of prep time.

Entertaining guests is not inexpensive. Even if the guest treats your family to dinner out one night, be advised that your grocery bill will expand exponentially with the number of people and the length of time they are in your home. Count on spending lots of $$$ on food.

If menu planning is a murky muddle, head for a big box store or your favorite super market and pick up just about anything you will need to feed people for anywhere from a weekend to a week. Ready-made dips, hors de oeuvres, and special meat and fish platters abound along with fresh salad selections and prepared dinners, fresh or frozen. Next hit the breads, desserts and wines; add a couple of nice cheeses and a large jar of mixed nuts, and you've finished the food portion of the visit in one shopping trip — poorer, but hopefully more relaxed.

I like to start with a roast beef or a ham that has the potential for leftovers that can transition into sandwiches or a casserole for other meals. Be forewarned, however. This doesn't always work. Once I baked a large ham and served up plenty of side dishes along with salad, rolls and a dessert. I ran off to a meeting, intending to eat my dinner when I returned. My husband greeted me at the door, clearly distressed. He told me that this family of four had eaten the entire ham without leaving a bite for me!

MORNIN' Y'ALL

"Morning has broken" and every household has its own family rituals and routines. Disrupt these daybreak rites and the ensuing host discomfort is apt to color the rest of the visit. The word from here is, the host probably needs to have the coffee pot set up and ready to go at the first blush of dawn. And the guest should have inquired about the acceptable time for appearing in the kitchen for coffee and breakfast. Wake up calls vary from family to family along with food served or made available.

Recently I entertained two women, my former classmates, for a week. I would get up around 6:00 a.m., feed the dog, empty the dishwasher, start the coffee, set the table for breakfast and put some muffins, coffee cake or cornbread in to bake. By the time I had showered, walked the dog, poured the juice and fried some bacon or sausages, and brought in the newspapers, it was 8:00. My guests then miraculously appeared, ready for breakfast. This routine was easy for me, and though I never set a time for breakfast, 8:00 seemed to work for my guests as well.

Another house guest (Well, Boorish Bob— again) made the morning meal less than comfortable. Bob's wife, my husband and grandson were all ready for breakfast by 8:00.on Saturday morning. We were kept waiting until Boorish Bob appeared at 9:45. He then shunned the bowl of fresh strawberries because they were sprinkled with sugar. Note: This is the guy who swigged down a full bottle of vodka and half a bottle of brandy (pure distilled sugar) in a brief four day visit. Contradictions are so much fun! I was at fault here. I should have fed everyone else and let Bob pick at the leftovers when he decided to honor us with his presence. Or, the night before, I could have announced, "Breakfast's at eight."

A warning to hosts and guests alike: Do not appear for breakfast in a bathrobe or, God-forbid, skivvies! Tiptoeing to the kitchen in a bathrobe for a cup of coffee to take back to one's room while preparing for the day is okay, but skivvies — NEVER!

Tom and Marion were shocked to have their guest appear for breakfast only in his underwear. The guest's wife mercifully shooed him back to the guest room to put on a shirt and pants.

It doesn't matter that less than this is worn at the beach. This is not the beach. This is breakfast time in your home with friends, family or acquaintances. Don't start the day by embarrassing yourself or your guests. I was annoyed one morning when I entered my own kitchen to find our guest drinking coffee and reading the newspaper in her sleepwear and bathrobe. As far as I'm concerned, a bathrobe is exactly that — a robe one puts on to scoot from bedroom to bathroom. It is not appropriate for dining — or even drinking coffee in the kitchen. Of course, if it's alright with you, then your rules supersede mine.

However, if you are in the habit of going into the kitchen in your underwear for morning coffee or breakfast, you need to change this pattern when you are entertaining houseguests. When small children or teenagers are the guests, it is especially important not to appear in a state of partial un-dress.

Many of us begin our day and relationships with those in the household with a warm "Good morning" greeting. Often the perfunctory conversational starter is "How did you sleep?" (Avoid this question if your guests have been relegated to less than comfy sleeping arrangements!)

Cameron and her husband had been invited to visit their friends Anna and Bruce Tagert in London where they had rented a flat for the summer. When Cameron bounced into the kitchen for breakfast the first morning after their arrival, her hostess was ensconced behind the London Times, sipping her coffee. Anna didn't even look up to acknowledge Cameron's presence. Discomfited, Cameron initiated a "Good morning," Her hostess snarled that she didn't engage in conversation until after she had had her morning coffee.

Cameron generously forgave her hostess, suspecting Anna had done herself in by inviting too many people in too short a time to join them during their vacation in London. Still, an attempt to initiate a pleasant beginning to every morning is the obligation of the host or hostess.

On the other hand, nothing is apt to raise a host's hackles quite like having his morning paper vanish before he gets to it. One host came down to his morning coffee and newspaper to find that the *New York Times* had vanished into the guest room. Grrrrr! At our house, we have three morning papers delivered, so there is plenty of reading material for everyone during morning coffee and as an assist in generating breakfast conversation. (Try to avoid political issues). While reading the morning newspapers and sipping coffee is usually a pleasant way to begin the day, many of us are jolted and disturbed when our reverie is disrupted by someone reading an article aloud or interrupting others while they are reading. Most of us beyond fourth grade prefer to read to ourselves. Even the kids want to read their funnies alone.

Whether morning appetites are ravenous or non-existent, the host should have comfortable morning menus in place for the duration of the visit. These may include: cereal, yogurt, bagels with cream cheese, smoked salmon and sliced onions, Muffins, store bought or made from a mix, fresh fruit and juice along with coffee and tea. Any number of breakfast casseroles can be assembled the night before and popped into the oven the following morning. Of course, ham, sausage, bacon and eggs — even omelets are sometimes in order, depending on the cooking fervor of the host or hostess.

I thoroughly enjoy preparing a scrumptious breakfast and setting a pretty table to enhance the food and conversation.

However, when your guests will be in your home for more than three days, everyone may be more comfortable if breakfast is less formal.

Ginny stocks her refrigerator with yogurt, muffins, bagels, juice and fruit. She then tells her guests to please pretend they live there and help themselves to what they can concoct from the fridge. Ginny leaves for the gym at 7:30 and will touch base with her company around10:00. This casual approach probably works best for both guest and host. Everyone feels more relaxed and comfortable. The host is exempt from undue hustle and bustle about food preparation and the guest is free to prepare his own and then eat when he is ready.

THE LUNCH BUNCH

Guests who go off on their own to explore the local attractions should be in charge of finding their own lunch. Some may choose to make a bag lunch before leaving, but it is a bit much to expect the host or hostess to provide this extra accommodation.

I keep cold cuts, cheese and bread as well as fruit and veggies for salads that can be quickly turned into a lunch if the visitors are at the house for that meal. Ham, roast beef or corned beef left over from the first night's dinner are especially nice for lunches later in the visit. An au-juice mix will work with sliced beef on long rolls for French dip sandwiches. Most everyone likes ham and cheese sandwiches or any ground up cooked meat with onion and pickle relish moistened with mayonnaise make great old fashioned sandwich spread. Ruben sandwiches with layers of corned beef, Swiss cheese, and sauerkraut then lathered with Thousand Island dressing on rye bread are especially appealing.

Remember Boorish Bob? I had asked before he and his wife arrived if they had any food allergies or issues. Frances, his wife, said that she couldn't eat onions, but other than that, they had no problems. Well, one afternoon I had lunch on the table, and Bob leaned over the table and asked if there was mustard in the potato salad. I said, "There probably is. Why?" He announced that he was allergic to mustard. I then asked what happened if he ate mustard. He let me know that he would go into anaphylactic shock. By that time I was ready to find a list of dishes with concealed mustard and observe the symptoms of anaphylactic shock up close.

I sometimes make tea sandwiches ahead and store them in plastic bags covered with damp tea towels in a plastic shoe box in the refrigerator. These are ready for emergencies. There are many wonderful recipes for tea sandwich spreads on the internet via COOKS.COM.

Lunch is usually a casual meal when guests are around. Keep it simple and tasty. This is the meal that best lends itself to being eaten in odd locations: on the deck, a picnic in the park or at the beach, in the boat while fishing or rowing, on the hiking trail or even in a restaurant. Both host and guest can be creative about the location and the menu.

DINNER TIME, DEARS

A very long chapter on food has been deleted from this book because Teresa, my friend who is in the book business, let me know this is not a cook book. Thank her for relieving you of reading through all of my favorite recipes and menus for dinner parties. There is a whole world of cook books on the shelves of every book store and library, so Teresa is right, you don't need mine. Here are a few suggestions, though for simplifying the problem of serving more than one dinner for company.

Three hors de oeuvres with a glass of wine before dinner work well to help satiate big appetites. I like to serve a dish of nuts, one dip (home-made or purchased) with crackers and one other which might be a plate of cheese chunks and olives on toothpicks or perhaps a made ahead appetizer from the freezer. Shrimp seem to be a universal favorite.

Remember that most folks are purportedly watching their waistlines so fruit is often a good choice for desserts and as an accompaniment for both breakfast and lunch. Pretty napkins and a small vase with a flower or two brighten up the table and make any meal more fun.

Guests who imagine that the hostess is a human version of the "Do It All" appliance needs to revise their attitude. Meals are usually planned ahead and have a set time for being served. Eric and Josephine were frequently upset by a long-term house guest who more than once left the house to go shopping just before dinner was put on the table. They needed to wise up, and eat the meal without her in attendance as happened in the following example.

Lucy's daughter —in-law appeared in her jogging suit just as Lucy was finishing the dinner preparation. The daughter-in-law announced that she was going out for a short jog. Lucy said, "I'm just putting the spaghetti in the water." The daughter-in-law repeated, "I'm going out for a short jog." Lucy then dropped the spaghetti in into the boiling water as the daughter-in-law left the house. The rest of the family ate and the dishes were done and put away when the rude family member returned from her jog.

Good conversation and social interaction are apt to be generated around a table of good food. Probably somewhere in our long genetic past and entrenched in our DNA are ancestral behaviors that incorporate eating and conversing Therefore, a marvelous houseguest experience includes good food and plenty of it.

-seventeen-

Y'ALL LEAVE

"He thought he saw a Buffalo
Upon the chimney piece
He Looked again, and found it was
His Sister's Husband's Niece.
'Unless you leave this house' he said,
'I'll send for the Police"

"The Magic Locket"
<u>*Sylvie and Bruno*</u>
by
Lewis Carroll"

G randma Gates in Illinois says, "I really like the Comers and the Goers, but not the Comers and Stayer's." Most of us know that houseguests have a shelf life of three days or less. Host anxiety tends to set in when the time for guest departure has elapsed and the company is still taking up space and devouring groceries. If your guests are showing signs of prolonging the stay, then it is probably time for you to jump start the departure process.

With nary a twinge of guilt, lingerers openly vandalize the host family's time, territory and provisions. The Sicilian proverb: "The guest is lord of the house" has its limits no matter the culture or location on the planet.

A houseguest visit is, by its very nature, temporary — or should be. Guests, who delayed leaving my home in a timely fashion, left strained relationships that prompted the writing of this book Even though lingerers may fully understand when their welcome is worn out and that the family nerves and resources are shredded, they boldly extend the visit because they believe they have territorial rights under the roof of a "gracious host."

Ann and her physician husband, Carl, lived in Walnut Creek, California and vacationed at their second home in Ocean Beach just outside San Diego during the summer.

One summer, Anne invited her friend Shirley and her six kids to join her and her brood of five for a week until Ann's husband, Carl could join his family for his own brief vacation. Well, eleven kids for a week is bound to involve a few stressful moments even in a carefree ocean setting. Shirley threw a fit when two nine year olds engaged in a watermelon seed spitting contest while Anne thought this was a fairly normal game for nine year old boys. Then Anne commented that Shirley had allowed the kids to eat some cookies that Anne was saving for dessert one night. Ever after, Shirley bought snacks only for her children and kept them in her room. Finally, Carl came down to vacation with his family. Shirley and her six kids stayed on. Anne mentioned that she thought Shirley and her children would leave when her husband arrived. Shirley's response was, "It isn't worth it to drive all this way for only a week." She stayed for three weeks!

Shirley overstepped multiple boundaries and forty years later her transgressions are still vivid in her hostess' memory. Anne was remiss by not establishing firm arrival and departure times for her guests. Shirley probably understood that her status had become that of an intrusive pest, but her strong personality coupled with tenacity won her large family extra freeloading vacation time in a very desirable location.

Dawdling may be a signal that the guests are intending to spend more time in the guest quarters than was originally planned. They might even say, "We'd like to stay on a few more days — or until tomorrow." This can become another instance where the host allows himself to be taken advantage of and becomes hostage to his own hospitable impulses and training.

If you do not want your guests to extend the visit, you must be certain they understand this. Since many guests arrive by plane, it is best to always ask them to forward a copy of their itinerary. If they have not booked a return flight, this will be apparent and you can confront this problem and insist it be solved well before they arrive.

> *One couple was scheduled to leave Wednesday morning after a three day visit. They needed to rent a car in order to drive to a conference in a nearby city. Upon learning that the conference center was closer than they had originally thought, they willy-nilly decided to stay through Thursday. They finally rented the car Friday morning, but then decided to stay until after lunch. The host had previous plans to meet friends for lunch at the country club. The lingering male guest (Boorish Bob) was a clear freeloader, he even wrangled an extra free lunch at the club. It is obvious that this couple was determined to save money by hanging on after their expected departure date and time*

Merunisa refers to these lingerers as opossums because she recalls having one of these critters take up residence in her small porch/den. When she tried to sweep the brute out with the broom, he simply played dead; the more she swept, the deader he played. Often lingerers play the opossum game — Leave? Huh? Why?

> *Miriam invited an elderly gentleman friend to spend holidays with her family. Inevitably, he stayed too long, so she packed up his suitcase for him, put it by the door and told him that it was time for him to leave.*

There may be, on occasion, legitimate reasons for guests to stay past the agreed upon departure time and date. Valid excuses might include terrible weather, a cancelled flight or acute illness. However, when guests tend to postpone leaving without extenuating circumstances or an extended invitation, what is a polite host to do?

During the olden days in the South, when it was customary for family to show up and stay for a month or two, a pineapple placed in the guest bedroom was the symbol of welcome. It was used again as a polite signal for guests to depart. Apparently it was tacitly understood and guests then made their polite leave taking. Someone suggested a needlepoint sign hung on the guest bedroom doorknob stating, "Don't mistake endurance for hospitality."

Battle-worn hosts have come up with lots of ideas and strategies for protecting the home turf. When frustration begins to rise, the most accommodating hosts might resort to unpleasant behavior, with the offending party being totally unaware of why the host is behaving this way. A fed up host might just stop the supply of fresh linens and towels, avoid preparing or supplying meals, and become cool to any social intercourse. A refusal to initiate conversation or provide only monosyllabic responses to a guest's small talk might work — or it might not! By the time guests have overstayed their welcome long enough, the host's communications might become terse responses through clenched teeth. If, however, the lingerer is determined to remain entrenched in the guest quarters, don't bank on any passive aggressive tactics to be effective.

Sometimes guests will, at the last minute, attempt to negotiate a departure beyond the original agreed upon date and time for leaving and often these tenacious folks have an array of flimsy excuses to delay leaving. Unless the host's ego is being massaged out of all proportion to his need for privacy and frayed nerves, he needs to say, politely or not, "No, that won't be convenient." We have other plans, so we have to say goodbye now." Mean what you say. If the hemming and hawing continue, just quietly and firmly repeat the statement. Then continue to reiterate this mantra and offer to help take his luggage to the car or to the train station or call a cab for the airport or any other conveyance out of your living quarters.

The host's plans are not the business of the guest. The head of the household, i.e., the host, is charged with protecting his family as well as himself. Though it may difficult for the host to assert himself and let the guest know that the visit is over, that is exactly what he needs to do. It is time to challenge the person who appears to have taken up permanent residence.

One frequent uninvited guest to our home, who happens to be a distant relative, has the unnerving habit of staying on and on. After her last departure, I wrote her a letter asking her not to give us any more gifts. She apparently felt that by loading us up with bizarre unwanted gifts that she was "paying her way." She called and wanted to know if she had done something wrong. I simply said, "Ten days is a long time."

Edna who lives alone and has a job in downtown Los Angeles, relented and allowed her sister, Audrey, to come and stay with her in her apartment until "her life straightened out." For awhile, Audrey paid rent and took Edna to work because they both had jobs in the same building. However, Audrey had to be at work an hour earlier than Edna, so Edna soon stopped riding with her sister. Within two months, Edna had decided that Audrey's visit had lasted too long and proved to be much more expensive and disruptive than Edna had imagined. Finally, Edna told her sister that she would have to leave and gave her a departure date and time. The month before she left, Audrey punished her sister with the silent treatment and communicated by slamming doors. Edna said she was bathed with relief the day she came home and found Audrey had gone,

Edna made the mistake of issuing an open-ended invitation. The lesson or rule is "no open-ended invitations." Never say, "Stay with us until you finish school" or "Stay until you find an affordable place to live."

Often guests, who are made aware of having over-stepped the boundaries, will respond with convoluted excuses. When confronted about their departure time, they may employ delaying tactics. These ploys may include excuses such as:

"We had planned to leave today, but . . .,
It's so nice to be with you, I'm sure you wouldn't mind . . .,
We will leave when the weather . . ."

Any old excuse will do since most hostesses are unprepared to deal with it on the spur of the moment. On occasion a guest might suddenly develop an illness—or even an emotional breakdown hinting that there is no where else to go during this crisis.

Each experience must be evaluated on an individual basis. If this is more than you and your family bargained for, put on your thinking cap and find other accommodations for the "patient" or send him home.

When you want the visit to end, remember the magic word, "Let." "We are going to 'let' you leave tomorrow morning. We are going to have lunch and then we will 'let' you be on your way." There is no need to explain your plans. You might add, "Just strip the bed and leave the sheets and towels next to the washing machine. We have a busy schedule for the day, so we will say 'goodbye' now. The door will self-lock when you leave."

The polite regional expressions, "Come back when you can stay longer." Or "Y'all come back, hee-ah?" are in the same category as those initial invitations that may have precipitated the visit in the first place. Do not say, "Come again," unless you are a glutton for unintended houseguest visits. If you wish to remain friends, but really prefer not to have this person return as a houseguest, refrain from accepting an invitation to his house. Rather, attempt to make arrangements to stay at a hotel when you visit his city or meet him in another place where everyone can pay his own hotel bills.

Roger's wife's friend, Monica, was getting a divorce; she didn't have much money and needed a place to stay for a while. Roger and his wife agreed that she could come and live with them for two months. A year later, Roger said, "Monica, you're going to have to leave, I want my house back."

During a brief conversation with Pam who lives at the beach, she shared that she no longer entertains houseguests. When I asked her why, she said that she felt she had paid her dues as a hostess. She went on to tell me that one year two or three families were vacationing at her home when she decided enough was enough. She poured herself a stiff drink, gathered everyone together and told them it was time for them to leave. With that courageous decision to re-establish and protect her boundaries, she forever ended her role as doormat hostess..

As their overstaying guests rolled out of the driveway Al and Valerie were bidding them farewell through gritted teeth and pasted smiles. They were waving and calling out: "Good riddance' good riddance." This backfired, shortly thereafter, when invited dinner guests were departing and Al and Val's own children began exclaiming, "Good riddance!"

A FINAL NOTE TO THE HOST:

GUILT ON YOUR PART IS NOT PART OF THIS TRIP.

Learn from the experience and be happy with yourself. For those who have had an overextended or unexpected houseguest experience and absolutely do not want a reoccurrence, it is time think about your turf and sanity.

SOME POSSIBLE TIPS TO HELP MANAGE OR HASTEN GUEST'S DEPARTURE:

1. "We hadn't planned on your staying this long and we have other events on our calendar. You will have to find other accommodations for the remainder of your visit." Provide these folks with a list of hotels or motels in the area.

2. Give the maid two weeks off before the visit so the potential guests can stumble through your clutter. Note: this may not deter some folks who live like this anyway.

SOME TIPS TO AVOID ENTERTAINING HOUSE GUESTS

1. Plead no guest room or quarter. "We have no room to accommodate guests"

2. "If you are visiting our city, call after you are settled in your hotel. Perhaps we could meet for dinner." (Or whatever seems easiest).

3. Make eight dogs and twenty-one cats permanent residents of your home. This is enough to dissuade most inveterate visitors.

4. Always have, or pretend to have, a full calendar that precludes entertaining people from out of town.

5. Simply communicate: "We have a policy of staying in hotels when we visit and we expect those who come to our town to do the same. Would you like a list of our local hotels?"

-eighteen-

THE SHODDY AND THE SHOCKING

"Unwelcome are the loiterer, who makes
Appointments he never keeps;
the consulter, who asks advice he never follows;
the boaster who seeks for praise he does not merit;
the complainer, who whines only to be pitied;
the talker, who talks only because he loves to talk always;
the profane and the obscene jester, whose
words defile;
the drunkard, whose insanity has begot
the better of his reason;
and the tobacco-chewer and smoker, who poisons the atmosphere
and nauseates others"

Anoymous

*I*t is usually assumed that hosts and guests share the same
goal and both contribute to the joys of a successful satisfying holiday. Many of us hosts who have jumped through
the hoops with high hopes of enjoying a grand old time, have
learned the hard way that the visit, more often than not, can be
dominated by an over-stepping guests.

These boundary breakers who disregard the basics have
snared their hosts in an uncomfortable web of bondage and
expect the host to maintain a courteous gracious demeanor.

We were inconvenienced and annoyed when Boorish Bob
disconnected our telephone line in order to use his computer

for lengthy periods of time while he was a guest in our home. It is wrong to assume that the host's life is at a total standstill while visitors are present and that the host needs to sacrifice his own amenities for the guest's convenience.

Another time we had a guest who asked to use our computer. We have important private records on our computer, so we had it set up with a "Guest" access mode. This person came to me and asked for the code to access my husband's side of the computer because he felt the side designated to the guest didn't work for his needs. This man put me in an uncomfortable position. He needed to find a store with a commercial computer outlet and process his business there.

Candice always hides her jewelry when guests are invited for any length of time. While she is reasonably certain that family and close friends are not security risks, she is ambivalent about strangers, friends of friends or friends of relatives. In fact, Candice has lost quite a few valuable pieces of jewelry. Candice suspects that her son's friend ransacked her possessions bit by bit over several visits with the theft going unnoticed until quite a number of jewels were missing.

Most of us aren't concerned about securing possessions until our privacy has been breached. When it is discovered that a trusted guest has defiled our personal territory, we feel violated.

Helen's husband's cousin visited from another state. After the cousin left, Helen discovered that the cousin had gone through her closet, tried on her clothes, tore the tags off new clothes and then left all in a heap on the closet floor. Helen confronted this relative about this blatant bad behavior by phone, and then let the rest of the family know that the cousin would never again receive a return invitation.

It usually doesn't occur to most of us to secure our personal papers and belongings before entertaining house guests. We are left with permanent shock when we open our homes to someone we have known for years, and presumed is trustworthy, only to later discover that our possessions are missing.

Viola and Kathy had a close relationship for many years, and Kathy had been an enormous help during Viola's divorce. After Kathy visited Viola, however, it became apparent that she had gone through all of Viola's private files. At one point, Kathy, a geriatric nurse who had taken care of a friend's elderly mother, let slip that she found out the sick woman was leaving her home to one of her sons. This was privileged information that could only have been acquired by going through the sick woman's private papers, so Viola's suspicions of Kathy as a dangerous snoop were corroborated. Viola, fed up with her belongings being rifled and feeling as though her hospitality had been desecrated, locked the files and hid the key on a nail in the back corner of the linen closet. After Kathy left from the next visit — the key in the linen closet had vanished.

Viola had also committed the cardinal sin while playing host. She gave Kathy a key to her house. Somehow Kathy lost the house key and told Viola that she only had one key, but she couldn't recall what it was for. Viola took it to the locksmith's and, sure enough, it was the key to her old filing cabinet.

Viola's attitude is, "We all have flaws," and Kathy is her beloved friend. It became obvious, however that she needed to protect herself from her good friend's compulsive snooping. Viola found an article by "Dear Abby" about respecting boundaries. She left this piece of writing in a place where Kathy was sure to see it. Then, she first locked all of her papers in suitcases that she slid under her bed and later accessed new filing cabinets with very secure locks. She now carries those keys with her at all times. Viola has reported that Kathy has stopped visiting her, and she seems somewhat concerned that Kathy may have had her feelings hurt because of the "Dear Abby" article.

Thinking back, I was shocked, hurt and confused to learn that my own mother went through my closets and drawers while she was visiting me. This is the woman who was very strict about privacy issues. She died many years ago, but I have often wondered what prompted her to such uncharacteristic behavior.

Leslie, who had a small home and lived on the edge of poverty felt sorry for Sam who was between jobs and need a temporary place to stay. (Yes, Sam qualifies as a short-term refugee). Leslie was traveling for a few days and agreed to let Sam stay at her place for the short period that she would be out of town. When she returned to her home, she discovered a hole in the ceiling where the decorative hanging rattan chair had hung. Apparently, Sam had decided to sit in it and pulled the ceiling down with his weight. She found her microwave open and splattered with a take-out spaghetti dinner that had exploded while being heated. Most unsettling of all, she had left a gas credit card (unused and pretty much forgotten by her) on a shelf in the bathroom. It had vanished. Even though she immediately cancelled the card when she found it was missing, the following month she knew that she had been defrauded by Sam when she received a bill for the charges he had applied to the card.

One guest to our home wanted to know where we kept our trust and other papers of a personal nature. We simply told him that other family members had them.

Medicine cabinets, all closets, drawers, filing cabinets, jewelry, credit cards, keys, check books and computers need to be secured when some guests will be occupying the house.

If anyone asks to use the computer, then it's fine to say, "Our computer has personal files so we don't allow other to use it." Then, "let" the guest know where to find a computer outlet store. There is no need to apologize for protecting privacy. If you are more liberal about sharing the computer, use passwords to protect your files.

Smoke Gets In Your Eyes ...

And nose, clothes, furniture, drapes, and bedding; it seeps into cracks and crevices, it turns the mirrors a filmy yellow; it turns white walls ecru. And secondary smoke is now known to cause physical damage to those in the vicinity. Smokers STINK! Of course, we all stink to someone — but unless the smeller is another smoker, the distinctive smokers stink is horrible! Just as those who share their residence with eight dogs and twenty-one cats and are impervious to the fact that their home reeks of animal urine and other acrid smells, smoker's olfactory nerves have adapted to the choking stench of their smoldering habit.

Those guests who happen to be smokers need to automatically take their nasty habit out of doors without being told. Yes, I am a reformed smoker and I tend to harbor all the fervor of those who have experienced an epiphany and are intolerant of smoking. As a kid, I had a close friend whose parents were chain smokers and compulsive beer drinkers. This was my early introduction to the stale morning-after smells of a beer garden. Ugh. It's a marvel that my friend grew up healthy and a non-smoker or drinker.

> *Dianne and Sam were living in Minnesota. When they entertained guests during the cold Christmas season, Dianne told the smokers in the company that they were not allowed to smoke in the house. These folks dutifully bundled up and went out in the 10 degrees below zero weather to blow smoke. Dianne shared her story with neither a twinge of guilt nor regret for maintaining her household standard.*

For those of us who don't smoke or gave up the habit long ago, the dependence on a little white roll of paper and plant material is illogical. In the not so far past, most households had at least one smoker. Some argue that the habit is atavistic, harking back to the Indians passing around the peace pipe. I have to admit that many smokers tend to have out-going personalities and are fun to be around. However, residual smoke in a household of non-smokers is offensive. Any guest with a smidgen of sense will understand that smoking in the house of a non smoker is not done.

It's your turf. If you don't want your house guests to smoke in your home, tell them! We recently entertained a guest for a week. She is a smoker and I unfortunately reverted back to my "doormat" days. I told her that she was welcome to smoke at the kitchen table as long as she burned a candle and left the back door open. The next thing I knew, she was smoking upstairs in the bedroom and the bathroom. I was in the downstairs master bathroom and I could smell smoke. It zipped right on down through the lath, plaster and wood to invade the most private corner of my home.

Pricilla was entertaining her college roommate, Helen, from the opposite coast. She knew that Helen was a smoker, so she told her in advance of the visit that she (Helen) would be expected to smoke outside. Pricilla went upstairs one day and discovered Helen smoking; she reminded her guest that she was expected to take her cigarettes out doors. Helen haughtily replied, "You didn't even know I was smoking until you came upstairs."

Guests who are smokers need to observe strict rules of smoking outdoors and keeping their habit from bothering the home family.

BOOZERS

Excessive alcoholic consumption is apt to be another issue arising during a house guest visit. An open bar can certainly look inviting to a person who may be classified as an alcoholic or who might be medicating symptoms of some underlying mental or physical illness. Alcohol as an anesthetic may soothe the soul of the drinker or release his inhibitions, but his imbibing may also serve to annoy, irritate or trouble his companions.

A couple of years ago, we entertained an old friend of mine and her new husband. He was a retired college administrator. (You guessed it! Boorish Bob) With his string of academic credentials, we were expecting a sophisticated house guest who would share our interests in the theater and join us for a couple of parties. We weren't prepared for his inordinate interest in the booze laid out in our dining area. In a period of four and a half days, he managed to drink a full bottle of vodka and a half bottle of expensive brandy. He was clearly confused and not quite happy when my husband refused to join him in an extended after dinner drinking spree. "Hey, it's time to party!" My husband responded with, "Enjoy yourself, I'm going to bed."

Another evening we were watching a film that featured my friend's former colleagues. After downing several drinks, Bob sprawled across a sofa and proceeded to snore his way through our entertainment. When his wife interrupted his sleep by shaking him and saying, "Bob, don't you think you should go up to bed?" He responded, "Oh, no, I'm listening." Whereupon, he would throw back his head and once again begin his loud snoring.

Boozers are a blight on any polite social gathering. For anyone to get sloshed and spoil a party is abominable. There's a double whammy when it's done at the expense of the host. Sensitive house guests observe and adopt the behaviors of the host family with regard to alcohol. In our case, when we have company, we generally offer a couple of drinks before dinner, a couple of glasses of wine with dinner and then offer an after dinner drink. Anything beyond this is considered excessive. Bob was pouring himself several drinks before dinner and than filling brandy snifters half full a couple of times after dinner – only to revert to vodka after the brandy. While we are generous with our food and drink, we are uncomfortable with excessive alcohol consumption. Guests who drink this much in a short period of time should replenish the host's bar with a bottle or two, but don't count on it!

If you do not drink alcoholic beverages and don't allow it in your home, it may be a good idea to so inform your guest when issuing an invitation. If you have made this clear, guests should not presume it is okay to bring their booze into your home. Alcohol is offensive to many people.

In the long ago, my family always celebrated holidays with plenty of alcoholic cheer. However, one of my father's friends was a recovered alcoholic. If his family was included with other guests, all alcoholic beverages were put away. Other friends and family who were on the guest list were informed that there would be no alcoholic beverages served and told the reason why. No one ever seemed to mind, and some of these alcohol-free holiday celebrations were among our most memorable. Smoking and excessive drinking can upset your plans for a happy visit.

COUTH AND CONVERSATION

Comfortable manners around a table of good food often create the setting for warm conversation that helps make a houseguest visit memorable. When basic conventional protocol is breached, dining companions are left aghast. Most of us know that everyone waits to begin eating until everyone is served. It is acceptable to begin eating only if the hostess is busy and asks folks to start without her.

Bernice and Jerry Godfrey were entertaining friends, Sabina and Albert, from South Africa for several weeks. During their stay, the two couples were invited the host's friends to a private dinner party. The hostess was busy putting the food on the table when, Sabina, who is a well-to-do business woman, promptly sat down and began eating—ignoring the fact that others were waiting until everyone was served. Sabina had finished her meal before the hostess was able to seat herself at the table.

Bernice and Jerry were, of course, embarrassed by this self-indulgent self-centered discourteous behavior; this social offense still rankles when the memory of it surfaces.

In the same vein, Daniel told me about a more flagrant violation of manners.

> *He was brought up in the country in Arkansas. His father was paralyzed and wheel chair ridden, his mother worked in the chicken factory; there were five children to feed. If the family was going to eat, it was Daniel's job to go out and shoot dinner. An uncle was visiting and one of the teenage sisters had made tortillas and set them on the table for the family dinner. The uncle came to the table, seated himself, ate all of the tortillas and then left.*

This has to be one of the most egregious examples of dreadful behavior that has ever come my way. This is a sharing family, living at the poverty level; the uncle, who should have understood the circumstances, thoughtlessly ignored the work of a young girl who prepared the food for the family. Gluttony and bad manners coalesced to leave these young people painfully hungry.

Using cell phones shouldn't have to be mentioned as a huge violation of manners at any dining table. But guess what, we took a guest to dinner at a friend's house and while we were seated at the table, our guest and the host started talking about a friend they had in common. The guest promptly jumped up, grabbed her cell phone and dialed the number of the third party friend who lives on the other side of the country. I was appalled. I sat quietly wondering why anyone would do such a thing. Finally, I decided that our guest was attempting to form a more intimate bond with the host family and the friend on the other end of the line. Just as when we attend the theater or any public performance, every diner should turn off his cell phone and call or retrieve messages later in private.

My personal view is that cell phones should be turned off before entering another person's home, restaurants, stores, theaters and the gym; all of these need to be designated cell phone free areas. Others do not want to be forced to listen to your private conversations. Further, many cell phones are now also cameras and often become a matter of serious concern for others who do not wish to be photographed.

When a fervent Democrat is seated across from a rigid Republican at your dinner table, duck; switch subjects — the weather might do as a cooling topic — unless, of course, it happens to be global warming and could result in conflict. It is necessary to avoid introducing any belief that can be contradicted whether political, religious, or financial. The world is full of marvelous topics for discussion; it is always best to discuss an unarguable subject.

> *One evening after dinner with houseguests, when the kitchen was cleaned Bruce, Valerie and their two guests were ready for a quiet conversation when a political discussion erupted. It rapidly became a shouting match among the two guests and Bruce. They had enjoyed a convivial day and dinner together. The acrimonious diatribes undid all of it.*

Though it has been my observation that folks tend to hold more tenaciously to their parents political stance than their family's religious heritage, it is still best to side-step both pious and impious personal positions. Particularly during an election period, it might be wise to have a couple of signs posted on the coffee table and again on the dinner table, _Politics Not Spoken Here_. The suggestion may appear as a joke, but wise guests and hosts may well appreciate the relief from biased opinions from either side of the political spectrum.

During one houseguest visit, Lois had a difficult time biting her tongue when a well educated man with a prominent position held forth with one of the most ignorant diatribes she had ever had to sit through. This man denounced one particular religion and fervently proclaimed that all of their religious shrines needed to be decimated. Lois could only deduce that his hate was born of irrational fear and ignorance.

Dinner is spoiled by guests with such entrenched views spouting malicious attacks.

Money as a conversational dinner topic is another huge NO-NO! Our finances are personal. There is never any need to let anyone know how much money one earns, how or where it is spent or invested. If a visitor or guest thinks he is somehow included in the other person's financial dealings as potential customer or heir, it should be discussed privately and only if necessary. There is no need to publicly find out that you may be quite disappointed. Attempting to solicit money for charitable foundations or other enterprises has no place in any houseguest conversation. Fishing for funds must rank as the ultimate in bad manners.

One man who supposed he was the heir of an elderly gentleman told him that he had two choices, "You can stop spending so much money or you can die." The hostess (the wife of the elderly gentleman) managed to maintain her equilibrium, but later she shocked this man by letting him know that her husband had no long-term health insurance and a nursing home stay of any length would eat up any hopes of inheritance.

Some people best identify themselves by discussing their current or even past malady. This topic may engage an audience for a minute or two, but usually becomes either offensive or boring. If the sufferer has no immediate crisis, then there is no immediate need to rush to ER or call 911; the subject needs to be dropped. Questions and discussions of personal health issues should be avoided.

Carolina was shocked one evening when their guest launched, during dinner with other invited guest, into what she considered to be a comic description of her recent colonoscopy.

Folks who have undergone medical tests or surgical procedures of a personal nature usually prefer to keep these experiences to themselves. Listeners also prefer they remain private.

Sometimes there is a guest who, rather than engage in conversation, initiates a spree of joke telling. An occasional joke that enhances the conversation with anecdotal lightness and fun can certainly enhance the conversation. Sometimes, though, it is difficult for some of us, to respond to a series of jokes that are out of context with the current conversation. My view is that these folks are bereft of conversational topics, and represent a definite blot on the dinner conversation.

On occasion there is a true living room comedian whose humor is great fun; these people can be jewels as guests. However, not everyone appreciates extemporaneous clowning as a substitute for conversation, so these jokers need to keep their performance at a minimum. Their comedy routine should use the current conversation as a framework for their theatrical performance. Your living room is not a little theater and out of context sketches are reminiscent of Junior High dramatic monologues. These really are okay if the actor is in the eighth grade. It is up to the host to change subjects by introducing a new area for discussion.

One frequent houseguest of ours, who is brilliant and in possession of a Ph.D, frequently launches into an ear splitting screech at periodic intervals, sometimes followed by baby talk. I suspect she is seeking the attention of everyone in the room; all eyes are then focused on the screecher. I surmise that she was brought up in a noisy household and this behavior simultaneously supplies her with some sort of adrenaline rush and provides her with the view that she is embellishing the party. Raucous tones are at once grating and unnerving for those who are less that totally deaf.

BIG BAD BLUNDERS

Some houseguest misbehaviors are so extensive and egregious that it is difficult to even analyze the stories and file the various gaffs and outrageous conduct under appropriate chapters. Since most of the offensive folks represented here are beyond the age of twenty-one, the term "mature adult" is the ultimate oxymoron.

At times we invite people who don't live up to who we thought they were. (Did we change or did they? Perhaps it was both of us!) If guests aren't friendly, reluctant to participate in planned activities, don't show respect for your territory, are demanding, or fail to appreciate the effort you have expended to make their stay pleasant, then it's time to re-evaluate your relationship and your guest list.

A mélange of manipulative, controlling, unbalanced disruptive actions foisted upon well intentioned hosts can jeopardize the visit and even damage long-term relationships. Somehow, it is universally expected that the host will maintain a polite stance when guest behavior is woefully out of line. Cheer up; you can usually eliminate the worst ones from your next invitation. You are not a doormat. Let your guests know if they have overstepped any of the following boundaries:

1. Arriving with no invitation.
2. Arriving before the designated time.
3. Extending the visit beyond the departure date.
4. Asking to borrow your car.
5. Arriving with an extra uninvited guest whether it be an adult, child, or pet.
6. Expecting you, as host, to provide all and do all.
7. Refusing to join in planned activities.
8. Using a cell phone in the vicinity of the hosts or at the table
9. Tying up your phone line with his computer.
10. Acting out in the manner of a sexual predator.
11. Engaging in inappropriate conversation, joke telling or comedy routines.
12. Violating basic table manners.
13. Snooping
14. Stealing

Finally, we all need to remember that if everything goes perfectly, there are no good stories! Entertain with joy, verve, and comfort along with well established boundaries.

-nineteen-

HOUSE GUESTS FROM HEAVEN

"Granny's come to our house,
And ho! My lawzy-daisy!
All the children round the place
Is ist a-runnin' crazy!
Fetched a cake for little Jake,
And fetched a pie for Nanny,
And fetched a pear fer all the pack
That runs to kiss their Granny!"

"Granny"
by James Whitcomb Riley

When I told my swim buddies at the YMCA that a chapter in this book was being devoted to house guests from heaven, Diane K. cracked that these must be the ones who died. Really, when was the last time you entertained a houseguest who enthusiastically cleaned the kitchen, picked up a dust cloth or vacuum, or asked where the cleaning supplies were hidden so s/he could give the bathroom a thorough cleaning?

Anytime a conversation is opened about a house guest experiences, those enlivened by the heavenly ones are, indeed few and far between. They do occur though. There are some wonderful people who are always a pleasure to have in one's home. The Joie de Vive of each of these beautiful souls makes their company a satisfying experience. They usually project a casual attitude, have many interests, and often have a great sense of humor along with a generous spirit. They are good conversationalists, helpful, and are able to connect the dots in understanding family relationships and routines. They have a sense of when to interact and when to separate themselves from the host family.

Margo and Clifford Schupp are a fine example of Heavenly Houseguests. They are not only trustworthy, but also follow all of the guidelines for perfect house guests. They picked up and cleaned up after themselves and left the house in perfect order. They also followed up with a thank you note and a gracious invitation to their host family for a return visit. Margo and her husband told us how it was accomplished:

Several years ago an invitation to attend a wedding of Jehovah's Witnesses (in North Carolina) was extended to my husband and me. As we live in West Virginia, an overnight stay was necessary. We met everyone at the rehearsal where the groom-to-be handed us a key with a note from the folks with whom we would be staying. Our host had been called away to an out of town business meeting, however, and they wanted us to feel welcome in their home and enjoy the wedding.

We had never enjoyed hospitality in such a beautiful home minus its owners, especially since we were unacquainted with the hosts. The four poster bed with its lovely quilt and the little steps was as luxurious to sleep in as it was inviting. The same quiet inviting atmosphere pervaded the entire house. We enjoyed the wedding as well as the accommodations. We, of course, left everything in good order, just the way we found it. We secured the key to the house according to the instructions. We also left a thank you note with our name, address and home phone number. It included an invitation to stay with us anytime they wanted to get away to wild wonderful West Virginia.

Mom's friend, Dot Judge, from Lansing, Michigan would get off the train with her overnight satchel, looking and sounding like Hazel in the comics. She was straight forward, funny, industrious, easygoing and — well —delightful! The kids loved to see her come, and my husband, who was often less than hospitable, took delight in her company. She would join any outing with verve; she interacted with the children; she dispensed her pithy wisdom, and she charmed us all. We always felt that her once a year weekend visits were much too brief.

Jean Allen who has traveled the world as the wife of an executive wrote about her own recent happy houseguest experience: She recently had the privilege of entertaining two missionaries she had met in Monte Carlo thirty-three years ago. They were with Trans World Radio and during the post World War II period. They were broadcasting in over thirty languages from a facility built by Hitler that could reach beyond the Iron Curtain. They are both extremely talented and delightful people. The lot fell on Alex to preach the Sunday that Billy Graham visited. Sallie led the singing, while playing the guitar. They are ideal house guests because they have had a lot of practice. Missionaries historically cannot afford luxury accommodations, so they generally stay with their donors.

They arrived early afternoon after a cell call alerting me about their ETA. They brought with them the special food that Sallie needed to control her allergies along with organic snacks for everyone. They were gracious about the fact I had only emptied three drawers and fixed a shared space in the closet. They enjoyed the walk on the beach after dinner, even though it was a rocky road to the sand and they understood when I lost our valet parking ticket and we had to wait until last to leave.

Alex wanted to swim in the Pacific Ocean. I don't know how he did it, but there was not a speck of sand left in the house.

Their only request was to see my two daughters and their families. Lori and Cheri were only eleven and fifteen when we moved to France. I invited Lori and Cheri's families over for a Bar-B-Que. It was a wonderful time sharing lots of fond memories. They laughed it off when the propane ran out and we had to finish by broiling the steaks.

Breakfast was uneventful except I learned after frying up a pound of bacon that Sallie was a semi-vegetarian. By then I was convinced that the only safe way to have breakfast was Mr. T's, so she could have a veggie omelet and he could have ham, eggs and pancakes, and I could have my favorite bowl of grits. They had already packed their bags and pulled the sheets off the bed and ready to depart after breakfast.

They are more than welcome to return. It will probably be four years before another furlough. I will look forward to it.

It should be noted that the missionary guests were comfortable courteous company, but also Jean was an especially gracious and accommodating hostess.

A neighbor of mine who has been inundated with many difficult house guests, and whose home seems to have a revolving door, has not led her to be a less than helpful guest. She recounted a visit to a brother's home and while there defrosted his freezer because it needed it and her hosts didn't have time to do it. "I always go out of my way when I'm the guest. Not everybody thinks this way or practices it."

Teresa, who is a marvelous fitness instructor at the YMCA shares the story of her saintly mother-in-law:

I have the good fortune to have every year my mother-in-law come stay with me part of every winter. Grandma Joan lives in Brunswick, Ohio and loves to get away from the worst of winter's snow and ice. It also is a chance for her to have some time with her grandchildren, my two sons. If you met her you would see that it truly is a blessing to have her visit. Grandma Joan is the daughter of Polish immigrants and seems to enjoy nothing more than being here with us and taking care of her family. During the three months she is here, she does the grocery shopping, helps run the kids around, folds laundry and best of all, cooks! All year we look forward to savoring traditional delicacies we have only when grandma is here. She regularly makes potato pancakes, kielbasa and salmon patties. My favorite is buttered cabbage; of course it's because she puts more butter in it than I would ever dare. She does all these things for us in a very gentle, quiet and unassuming way, all the while with a gift for chatter and an ear for gossip. Grandma has many stories from decades past, all told as if they happened last month. We both are older sisters in our birth families and are often able relate to each other the frustrations of younger siblings.

HEAVENLY HOSTS AND GUESTS DURING DISASTERS

Sharing one's home and provisions with guests who pitch in to help may develop an atmosphere that unites, bonds and creates great memories; often disaster brings out the best in people.

It must have been about 1980 when my mother got caught in the worst snow storm of the century. She was driving through Canada from northern Maine back to Lansing, Michigan. She was involved in four accidents in two days. The last mishap ended when she skidded off the road down into a gully; the car was stopped by a barbed wire fence. Aunt Dot, whom she had been visiting, had put big boots and extra blankets in the car, so Mom put on the boots, briefly warmed up the car and wrapped herself the blankets. She was just dozing off when a Canadian policeman knocked on the car window. A truck driver had spotted her go over the edge of the road. The policeman took Mom to the police station, a center of the storm operations, where folks offered to house travelers who were stuck in the snow storm. Mom was given a room by a couple, Louise and Dan, who both worked. Well, her visit was extended by the severe storm and its aftermath; my dear mother, who was an expert at household skills, cleaned house, did the laundry, baked, and cooked dinner. I'm sure these folks were delighted to learn that the stranger they had taken in was a house guest from heaven. Mom did mention that her hosts said they hated to see her leave. I can only speculate that Mom was extremely grateful to these folks and wanted to be helpful, but she was also probably keeping herself from being bored and wanted to show off some of her baking and cooking skills while enjoying an unexpected vacation.

For one memorable week, nature's histrionics reprieved Louise Young from normal daily routines. An unexpected ice storm tore through her community and its terrible force drew friends, neighbors and strangers together in a memorable bonding. There were no rules – just helping and surviving, so their house full of extemporaneous visitors resulted in the best ever week of memories.

> *By two o'clock Monday morning March 4, 1991, we began hearing trees falling, exploding transformers, sirens and sleet beating against our windows. By daylight, almost everyone in Monroe County was without power. No street lights or traffic lights worked. Hospitals turned on emergency generators. Schools and businesses closed. At night entire neighborhoods were dark. The television and radio stations (no newspapers were delivered) reported a catastrophe that would last at least a week and, for many, longer. Pockets of power existed, and our house was in one of those pockets.*
>
> *At 9:30 am on Monday, March 4, my eighteen year old son's best friend and his father arrived at our door. They had walked a mile and a half from their house. Their car was trapped in their driveway by a fallen tree. They were cold and had lost power during the night. They were searching for warmth. And so began the trek of storm victims to our house..*
>
> *By the end of that day fourteen people –friends of our son, their parents, and our friends –sought refuge at our house. Many of them brought food from their freezers and refrigerators. For a week I cooked (with lots*

of help) bizarre dinners. Recently defrosted raspberries, chicken breasts, defrosted hamburgers, defrosted casseroles, defrosted vegetables created a week's worth of weird pot luck meals. People slept on our beds, furniture, and floors, having brought sleeping bags, pillows and blankets. We had that critical commodity –heat! We also had a working television so all of us could watch the disaster unfold.

As businesses reopened, my husband and other people went back to work but came to our house after work to eat, shower and relax. Some additional people dropped in from their frigid houses for the day to do laundry, take showers, drink hot coffee in a warm house and eat meals with us. Some returned to their cold houses and slept in front of their fireplaces for the night, only to return in the morning.

Since school was out, our son's teenage friends used our house as a gathering place. They provided constant laughs. One afternoon my son and two friends showed up with somebody's grandfather's chainsaw, planning to chop up the two trees lying in our front yard. For me, this was the scariest moment of the week. The poem "Out, Out," by Robert Frost, flashed through my mind. I think I shocked those boys by standing my ground and forbidding them to turn on the saw. They gave in and put it in our garage. I locked the garage. Weeks later a crew of men from a power company in New Jersey sawed up those trees..

By Saturday of that week our guests had electricity restored and had left for home. Normality returned. I was sad to see it end. For a week we had played cards, answered our constantly ringing doorbell, provided heat, hot water, and laughed almost constantly. Aside from the chainsaw incident, I remember that week as one of the happiest I ever spent. It was noisy, busy, and uncomfortable, but it was also an experience all of us remember with smiles. The Ice storm, for us, will always be one of our warmest memories.

Houseguests from heaven glitter forever in the memories of caring hosts. The heavenly do everything right — and then some. They help without intruding, they join in without taking over; they are respectful of the host's time, territory, privacy, and possessions. They arrive and leave in a timely fashion. When things appear less than perfect, they tend to have a sense of humor (without being comedians). These people don't need to scramble for or wrangle an invitation; the door is always open wide for these angels.

The heavenly host understands, and appreciates that invited guests temporarily reshape the household routine. The host plans, make allowances for and looks forward to these limited disruptions. The host regards his time with his guests as his own mini -vacation even though it is within his own home, and welcomes the guests who should equally enjoy and appreciate the mini vacation.

twenty

A GUIDE FOR GRACIOUS GUESTS

*"The happy gift of being agreeable seems to consist
not in one, but in an assemblage of talents tending
to communicate delight ;and how many are there,
who, by easy manners, sweetness of temper and
a variety of their undefinable qualities, possess
the power of pleasing without the aids of wit,
wisdom, or learning, nay, as it should seem,
in their defiance and this without appearing
even to know that they posses it."*

Cumberland

*E*stablishing a reputation as a gracious guest begins with the invitation. If the invitation has been wrangled, if you have decided to just "drop in" or plead for refugee status until your life turns around, then you've started your visit all wrong. As set down in the chapter on invitations, the host decides to open his home for guests. Keep in mind, if an invitation has not been issued, there is no invitation. To assume that you will be extended an invitation because you are in the region or planning to be in the vicinity is a mistake.

While it is certainly all right to call and say, "We are in your area or planning to be in your neighborhood," this does not mean that the person at the other end of the line will want you as a house guest or feel obligated to offer a room and board during your sojourn in his backyard. He may extend an invitation, or he may not — that is his prerogative. I am as apt to say, "How nice, we would enjoy seeing you. Where are you staying?" Or worse — "We are just planning to leave town, perhaps we can get together the next time you are here." Too often, folks have assumed that because they will be there on business or for a conference, or they have a scheduled lay-over, guest rooms are theirs for the calling. They are not.

The phrase, "House guest from hell," and the old aphorism, "After three days house guests and fish . . ." have endured through the ages because a household can comfortably and happily undergo a shift in routine for about three days. After that the visit begins to fray.

No two people are in perfect alignment. When we decide to live with another person it takes awhile to adjust to a comfortable routine, establish a division of labor within the boundaries of the household and adjust to the habits of the other person. Even — or especially — when a new baby is welcomed into the home, the former residents take awhile to adjust. Therefore, a house guest may be planned for and welcomed, but by the third day conversation is usually depleted and is becoming stale, clutter is starting to take over along with the laundry, cooking chores begin to become a burden; the routine and rhythm of the household has been disrupted long enough for family members to begin to feel uncomfortable.

It is worth repeating; invitations are pre-planned and extended by the host. Inviting oneself is a serious breech of etiquette. When an invitation is extended verbally, it should be followed by a written invitation, setting down the dates and times for arrival and departure. The host should also set down any events that will be attended so you know what clothes and accessories to pack for your trip. A courteous host will ask if you have any food allergies or religious dietary restrictions.

Once you have accepted the invitation extended by the host, it is your turn to forward your flight or driving itinerary so the host is able to plan his own calendar around your arrival and departure dates and times.

If a verbal invitation has been extended to you, but there is no written statement from the host outlining the invitation, you might elect to write your own intent to the host. Just as the host follows up an invitation, this guest's note should establish the exact time of your arrival and departure, some of the entertainment activities you might like to attend, and whether or not you will need transportation.

As a gracious guest, you might write the following just to be certain everything is in order before appearing at the door.

Dear Peggy and John:

We look forward to our visit with you from the 24th to the 27th. We will be there at 5:00 on Friday and leave after breakfast Monday morning. We are driving our own car which will allow us to visit some places while you take care of your weekend chores. If you have any plans we should know about, please get back to us. Plan on us treating you to dinner at Charlie's one evening while we are there.

There is an implicit understanding that reciprocity is built into every house guest visit. Anyone accepting an invitation for that great gratis getaway vacation needs to know there is always a tacit quid pro quo imbedded in the proposal. If the invitee is reluctant to return the invitation in kind, then it is best to gracefully decline the offer—thus avoiding future responsibilities and embarrassment for not reciprocating.

Arriving before the expected time or departing at a time later than previously set down is ranked from ungracious to harrowing in almost any book of manners.

In this age of soaring gas prices, it is best to plan on driving your own vehicle. Unless the host absolutely insists upon meeting your flight and driving you around during your stay, plan on renting your own car at the airport where you can return it when you depart. The gracious guest never asks to drive the host's automobile.

A gracious guest brings enough money and has enough room on his credit card to assume most of his own expenses during his sojourn at the host's home. He will have the financial resources to take the host family out for a nice dinner and give an appropriate gift to the host and hostess.

It may come as a shock for visitors from outside the continental United States that the U.S. host does not pay for all of the guest's expenses. While the host may invite the guest to a special event and pay for the tickets, the guest takes care of his own tourist attraction expenses. Most middle-class Americans do not have a budget that will permit funding someone else's vacation. More often than not, the culture shift has necessitated a transformation from more generous hosting.

Immigrants to the United States quickly learn that the workday and family schedules are generally quite different from those in the old country. It doesn't mean that their new countrymen rejected the old forms of hospitality, but rather, that the new lifestyle is defined by schedules that requires family members leave for work or school early in the morning and return home in late afternoon or evening. There are no mid-day siestas. Families tend to eat a hurried breakfast, lunch at work or school, and eat dinner from 5:00 to 7:00. By nine or ten o'clock, North Americans, after a quiet evening, are ready for bed. Many immigrants come from cultures that sacrifice for their guests and often lavishly cater to their needs (real or imagined). When the American visitor returns home, he may reflect that his entertainment standards will fall far short, when the return visit takes place, of what he enjoyed abroad. The desire to continue the home country traditions probably still remain in his heart and intentions, but might be less than a host would like to offer or be expected by the guest.

Recently I met my Korean neighbor attempting to take a walk in spite of a bad back. When I asked her how things were going, she replied that she was expecting two nieces as houseguests the following day. I immediately said, "Great, let them take care of you." She responded, "You don't understand, they expect to be treated like guests." Confused, I asked if they were coming from Korea and she replied, "NO – Boston." Hmm, "So what's the problem?" She said, "They are American -Korean, and they expect to be treated with traditional Korean hospitality meaning that the host does everything and pays for everything." The stress of the pending visit was visible in my neighbor's face and may have been a contributing factor in her aching back. Traditional Asian hospitality and manners prevailed in this case even though both host and guests have been residents of the United States for many years. Many immigrants to the U.S. are overdue for a shift to hospitality modes that accommodate lifestyles and routines of their adopted country.

Tan, a Vietnamese woman, was expecting company from France. She was grousing because her husband insisted that she use the best sheets, which were way in the back of the linen closet, and that she cook all of the meals from scratch and then serve the food on the best china which had to be hand washed. It was obvious that she was feeling tired and burdened before the visit began. Tan's marriage is probably still conducted in the original Vietnamese mode because many American women might have told him to make the beds, and to prepare and serve the food himself so he could feel proud.

At no time is it okay for the guest to bring along another friend without first asking permission of the host. Almost nothing is as shocking and upsetting for a host who expects one guest and then has more than one visitor show up. It is a temptation to attribute this behavior to those "Twenty-Something's," but I have had guests past sixty just show up with a "special friend" using the great line, "I knew it would be okay with you." The host may graciously okay it this one time, but as a host, I'm mighty tempted to strike this ignoramus from future guest lists.

Though Leyla had never met Faiza, she agreed to have her as a house guest so she could attend an Ethiopian wedding in San Diego. Faiza brought her young daughter with her as well as a friend. Neither girl was included in the invitation. The guests' flight was delayed which caused Leyla to miss a very important opening of a documentary film that she had co-produced When the guests finally arrived, Leyla rented a car to take them around and show them the town. It was a busy weekend with many trips sightseeing around the city.

But then, out of the blue, Faiza announced that she was expecting a cousin who was to arrive from another city. Layla drove her to the airport to pick up this new person who, again, was not part of the original plan. She felt forced to do this because she did not want to disappoint the guests. After waiting four hours, the cousin failed to arrive. The next day Leyla, who neglected her family for the entire time the guests were around, tried to prepare lunch for her family before the wedding reception. It was then that Faiza announced that the new guest was now waiting at the airport to be picked up by the hostess. Leyla refused to pick up the girl because she had to care for her family before she left for the wedding. As it turned out, Leyla was induced – against her will—to the airport to pick up the girl anyway.

As hostess, Leyla, was disgruntled by feeling forced to make multiple trips to the airport and then being required to entertain three extra people who were uninvited and unexpected. Shamefully, Faiza never bothered to call or write and say "thank you." When asked why in the world she would put herself out for strangers as she did, Leyla admitted that she suffers with a clinical case of Advanced Doormat Syndrome.

Pamela provided another example of being shocked when her invited guest from Oregon arrived at her door in Carlsbad, CA with her two grandsons aged eight and ten. Pamela was irritated and mystified why her friend would do such a thing. Two uninvited children on the scene kept the two adults from enjoying the entertainment activities that Pamela had planned.

It should go without mentioning that an invited guest never appears at the host's home with an uninvited/unexpected visitor in tow. If you should be this presumptuous, the host has every right to turn both you and your friend away and suggest the local Motel 6 for your lodging. Neither is he obligated to feed an extra unexpected guest.

Unless your children and pets have been specifically invited, find someone to care for them at home. Not everyone is charmed by kids, cats, dogs, rabbits, turtles, birds, or lizards. That's right, often neither family nor close friends are eager to entertain children or members of the animal kingdom.

HOW TO LOSE FRIENDS AND IRRITATE PEOPLE: FREELOAD

Interlopers/freeloaders are the more fitting expressions for over-steppers who often view the host privileged to have them when they magically appear for the honor of their company. With current advanced technology including cell phones and computers, the actions of "Drop-ins and Interlopers" cannot be justified by the inability to communicate. In other periods of history and in other cultures, the spontaneous visit was often welcomed — even occasionally — expected. When roads were rough, transportation marginal, and communication was lacking the speed and efficiency of our current technological advances, visiting family and friends was a different matter altogether. In this modern time, the possibility that family, friends or acquaintances will throw open the doors, lay down the welcome mat and shuffle around the kitchen to prepare a meal for you is ambiguous at best. There is no excuse for surprising anyone with your presence. Don't flatter yourself that the target host will be overjoyed by your impromptu appearance. It is more than likely that you are continuing your own house guest from hell reputation. You have overstepped a major boundary. If you haven't been invited and are unexpected, by all means, be prepared to be rebuffed by your target host. Understand that it may be necessary for you to find lodging and food at a local hotel.

In the spring of 2008 when the U.S. economy was in a steep slide, a weekly magazine suggested "freeloading on friends" as a means of cutting back on vacation expenses. This was terrible advice. The targeted hosts are also struggling with their own budgets. Extra unexpected guests will most certainly not be welcome.

I had to bite my tongue recently when a young woman who teaches school nearby told how she was planning her vacation up the coast of California by stopping to visit friends (whom she imagines to have an open door policy for guests)on her way to visit with her mother. Once at her destination, she plans to use her mother's car to visit other friends in Humboldt County. This young woman harbors the fallacious assumption that others will provide bed and board so she can vacation inexpensively. I hope she takes some money with her, because some of these people may be "out of town' when she arrives and her mother's car may be out for repairs.

THE HOUSE GUEST HAS DEFINITE RESPONSIBILITIES

Obligations include arriving on time and leaving on time in accordance with the invitation extended by the host. The thoughtful guest should bring clothing appropriate to the events planned during the visit. He eats, or at least tastes every dish that is presented. He does not encourage controversial conversation. He keeps his personal belonging s in the space provided by the host. He is expresses his appreciation of the accommodations and the efforts extended by the host. He helps keep the visit pleasant by helping with some of the daily chores, making his bed, emptying trash cans, hanging up towels and tidying up the bathroom after each use. He takes the host family out to dinner at least once. He usually arranges for his own personal transportation during the visit and travels with enough money to cover these expenses. At the conclusion of the visit, he strips the bed and takes the towels and sheets to the laundry area. He makes sure that he has packed all of his personal belongings. He immediately writes a thank-you note to the host family when he arrives home.

If the host becomes noticeably very sick while you are vacationing in his home, it is probably best to make other arrangements for your stay in the area. Unless you can be of real help or are absolutely needed, during the dilemma, by all means leave as soon as you are certain the sick person in being properly cared for. To leave when a seriously sick host without care is unconscionable and to stay and be underfoot during the illness may well exacerbate the problem and strain the relationship.

When my second daughter was very sick, I would drive up to her cluttered cabin with my sleeping bag and park myself on her couch in an attempt to share her final days and hopefully make her waning life more comfortable. Her bedroom was right there so I could be alerted if she needed help in the middle of the night. I tried to keep my belongings next to the couch in one small corner.

Each morning, I would make a fire in her wood stove, fix breakfast, change her sheets and attempt to clean house before running down the hill to do the laundry and shop for food. Being a guest in a home where someone is terribly sick is especially difficult. Yes, even though I was her mother, I was in the role of guest and temporary care taker. It was her terrain and I walked on eggshells in an attempt to get it "right." Sometimes when we think we are helping, we are really annoying or getting in the way. Attempting to make a sick person comfortable in their own territory requires special attention. In spite of my own efforts to be a helpful guest and mother, I always fell short, so

I empathize with those guests who attempt their very best and then find themselves wide of the mark and subject to criticism.

A visit with my eldest daughter offered a very different experience. She and her husband have a large elegant home on five acres in a cool climate. Perfection in architecture and landscaping, creative comfortable décor, gourmet food along with expensive wines, is the standard. The guest sleeping quarters with bathroom is above and beyond any five star hotel accommodations. Note: this is the daughter who lived in a shanty during college! As a guest in this beautiful setting, I'm never quite sure of my position or what I can do to help while there. I try to set the table and take directions making elegant and complicated hors de oeuvres, but more often than not I have a fragile sense of self because my operating mode is more casual. I have a tendency to feel inadequate with all of this wonderful hosting. Of course, there is also the relationship issue, but that is a separate and individual subject left to the discretion of the people involved.

Sometimes house guests are required to perform unintended duties as illustrated by my experience during a recent overnight visit with my youngest daughter, Celeste. She lives with her son on and acre and a quarter in the mountains. This independent woman has two cats and a dog. One particular night, I was there in the role of house guest and caretaker mom because my daughter had undergone surgery and needed some help. I curled up on the couch in her bedroom to be close in case she needed something during the night. My grandson left the house for basketball practice the following morning at 4:30. At 5:00 a.m. my daughter hollered, "Mom, Saddam (the cat) has an animal in the back bedroom." Note: this giant Russian Blue uses the back shower as the "kill" room for his prey. I groggily stumbled out of a deep slumber and went to see what was happening. Celeste handed me a pillowcase on my way and told me to try and catch whatever it was. I managed to trap the animal behind the door next to the bedroom wall with the impatient cat and curious petite sheltie, ears up right, curiously and anxiously looking on. I managed to get the two domestic animals out of the bedroom and then shut the door. This action released the frightened adolescent jack rabbit that proceeded to bounce around the bedroom with grandma in pursuit. You know, I caught that scared little guy by wrapping the pillow case around him and then holding him tight in my arms until he could be released outside. Sadaam twitched his tail by the French door in disgusted feline fury at loosing his prey. Guests probably need to be prepared for odd emergencies.

If there is an accident of any kind that damages
the host's property, the guest needs to acknowledge the damage
and insist upon replacing or paying for anything broken,
soiled or damaged.

Three people reported that guests visiting their homes had dyed their hair in the guest bathroom and permanently damaged the bathroom floor. Is it too much to expect a guest to replace carpet or tile imbedded with dye that can't be removed? No! It is up to the guest to take care of coloring hair before leaving home or find a professional beauty salon in the host's area.

Automobiles don't like being driven by strangers; therefore, throughout this book it is emphasized that host's should with-hold the keys to their transportation. Guests should not expect to drive the host's car. If, however, a host lends you his car and you return it damaged in any way, the repair bill is YOURS! If the host does graciously lend you his car, the vehicle needs to be returned in mint condition, washed and cleaned inside and out and the tank full of gas.

The man and his wife who were assigned the room with the beautiful antique bed that broke from their vigorous sexual activity, needed to have that bed professionally repaired for the host. Note: This guy bragged that after the bed collapsed, they finished on the floor and then had the temerity to boast that he hadn't missed a beat. He did, however, complain about "rug burns" on his knees!

If a guest soils the linen, it must be stripped from the bed immediately and the hostess informed. Blood, vomit, urine or semen needs to be taken care of immediately. Most stains respond to a rinse with ice water before laundering with warm soapy water.

It is the guest's responsibility to take care of this matter and re-make the bed as it was originally presented.

If you are visiting with a child who is a bed wetter, it is imperative that you as parents bring along plastic or rubberized sheets to protect the host's bed. Mattresses and bedding are expensive and if damaged by a guest, it is his/her responsibility to repair, replace or pay for the damage. Yes, beds as well.

Before leaving, you need to remember to check the closet and drawers — and maybe under the bed — to be sure you isn't leaving anything behind. It is disconcerting for a host to have to wrap and mail forgotten items. People have left jewelry, umbrellas and once in the long ago, a friend of mine who was a new Naval aviator left his huge (about size 14) military boots at my parent's home in Lansing, Michigan. Of course, they thought this was hilarious; the humungous footwear was packed up and shipped to him.

The guest also needs to remember to strip the bed and take the used sheets along with used towels to the laundry area. Of course, a guest from heaven will ask to remake the bed for the busy hostess.

BATHROOM ETIQUETTE FOR GUESTS

The subject of dirty diapers left behind in the bathroom is addressed in the chapter on entertaining children. DON'T DO IT!

On the subject of trash cans, one hostess was horrified to find a bedroom wastebasket filled with used condoms after her guests departed. While it was good of the offending couple not to flush them down the toilet, they should be discreetly wrapped in plastic bags and dispensed in a covered outdoor garbage pail.

A house guest visit in no way resembles being a guest at a hotel. Yes, the hotel staff asks that the guests leave dirty towels on the floor so they can distinguish between the used and unused towels. You may be your parent's house, but you <u>always</u> hang up the towels to dry or take them to the laundry area and put them in the washer before hanging your own fresh ones in the assigned bathroom. It cannot be emphasized strongly enough that the hosts (even if they are parents, step parents or other relatives) are not maid service.

While teenagers may still sometimes hang their towels on the floor, twenty-something's and beyond have now crossed the line into adulthood and are expected to behave accordingly. Of course, this second group usually behaves pretty much like the teens and may leave bigger messes.

AFTER USING THE BATHROOM, EVERYONE NEEDS TO:

1. Flush and light a match or spray with a bathroom spray

2. Wipe up the sink after brushing teeth, combing hair or putting on makeup.

3. Wipe out the tub or shower

4. Wipe off the counter and mirror

5. Hang up towels and bath mat.

6. Empty the bathroom waste basket

These small chores take only a few minutes to perform and guests who observe them will begin to nudge themselves into the "Houseguest from Heaven" category.

There is even a bit of protocol for the back woods outhouse. It is about one in the cold northern climate that has extremely narrow dimensions. Open the large coffee can that is the toilet paper holder (protects it from the bears (pronounced " baa ahs"), pull off a piece of paper and wipe the spider web out of the hole; put the toilet paper back in the can before emerging. Wash your hands in the freezing cold brook before going back to the cabin. In the woods, flashlights are a "must" for the nightly trek to the facility. On the other hand, an old fashioned thunder- mug might be a better choice if there are scary nocturnal howlers out there. Empty your own slops in the morning — in the out-house hole, of course. Then gather up some water from the brook and rinse that china-pot clean.

Houses in some foreign countries, in some ships, and even in some homes here in the .U.S. there are extra plumbing facilities. The bidet, designed as a great bottom washer off-er is some-times used by unsophisticated Americans in foreign countries for washing socks and underwear. Without instruction on the use of this handy hygienic device (squat above and splash) the unsuspecting innocent needs to beware of the possible disruptive tendencies of some of these particular plumbing facilities.

George from the nether regions of Minnesota (not bidet country) was a junior executive with a major American company on a weekend yachting business trip to the Bahamas. George, anxious to impress a beautiful guest, appeared at the Saturday evening cocktail party attired in a beautiful new suit. Early in the evening, he made a trip to the bathroom, promptly urinated in the bidet, flushed and royally sprayed his new suit.

If it appears that the host family has failed in the obligatory standards for invited visitors, i.e., safe, clean space for sleeping and bathing, palatable food and a pleasant social scene, then the guest may suffer in silence or terminate the visit. A scathing denouncement of someone else's housekeeping or culinary skills is reprehensible and that only casts a bad light on the disparager. Leave politely and quietly. We are all different, but we need to maintain our own dignity and allow others to preserve theirs. One guest that was here for longer than was comfortable for us, criticized some of the food, made a point of telling me that I left the kitchen cupboard doors open and he almost poked out his eye. Once again this was the insufferable "Boorish Bob."

From time to time, guests may find themselves ensconced in an atmosphere that is uncomfortable or beyond endurable. When accommodations are less than pristine or downright offensive—or the emotional atmosphere of the host home is uncomfortable or negative, the guests may want to bolt. It is a wise guest who has a secondary back-up plan for visiting the area along with excuses for exiting the host's premises. If it appears that the host family has failed in the obligatory standards for invited visitors, i.e., safe, clean space for sleeping and bathing, palatable food and a pleasant social scene, then you, as guest, may suffer in silence or terminate the visit. You can pack your bags and seek other accommodations. Polite departure excuses are nice, but not necessary.

Excuses for leaving before the planned departure time might go something like this:

1. Thank you for your hospitality; we have decided to stay at Motel 6 for the remainder of our vacation because my allergies are acting up.

2. It's so nice of you to have us, but we have to move on earlier than planned because we have a problem that needs to be solved back at the ranch.

3. I feel that I'm coming down with a nasty cold. We need to find a hotel room some where so you and your family don't catch our bug.

4. We are being called back home on business.

   One man used this excuse when his wife, who had gone out to her aunt's before him, stood in the road and flagged him down before he arrived. She told him auntie was so dictatorial that she and the kids had to leave immediately or go crazy.

Any excuse that won't offend the intended host will do. Do give the host a gift and perhaps take the family out for a meal. It behooves the guest to meet his social obligations even if the host's home and accommodations have been a disappointment.

The hearty house guest experience is one in which both host and guest exercise essential obligation toward making the visit comfortable, relaxed and satisfying. Otherwise the visit will not be a mutually pleasant experience.

PREPARE TO BE THE GUEST

1. The guest arrives close to the time designated on the invitation or calls if there is an unexpected delay.

2. The guest leaves close to the time designated on the invitation. (Dallying isn't done – ever!)

3. The guest makes arrangements for his own transportation unless the host specifically indicates that other around town travel means are available.

4. The guest makes his bed each morning and keeps his assigned sleeping area tidy.

5. The guest hangs up towels in the bathroom after their use or takes them to the laundry area.

6. The guest wipes up the tub, shower and sinks after use.

7. The guest appears for breakfast fully clothed for the day. (No underwear or bathrobes in any living areas).

8. The guest participates in all of the activities planned by the host

9. The guest who visits for three or more days treats the host family to dinner at an upscale restaurant.

10. The houseguest strips the bed and takes the bed linen and used towels to the laundry area at the end of the visit. A thoughtful guest will ask for fresh sheets and re-make the bed for the host.

11. The guest, of course, replaces or pays for anything that he might break during the visit.

12. Since the host has set aside time, supplied a clean sleeping space, fresh towels, food and some entertainment for the guest; a host or hostess gift is in order. These gifts should be tasteful, sincerely given, and unsolicited. What is a thoughtful caring guest to do? It is probably best to take a close look at the host family' interests and go from there. The monetary value of the gift should equal the amount of tax one would have paid on a hotel room. This is somewhere between $10.00 and $20.00 per day. A five day visit means a gift that would cost between $50.00 and $100.00. Yes, this is in addition to paying for the dinner at a fancy restaurant. The host is not underwriting your vacation.

Gift Suggestions for the Host/ess

I. Gift certificates lead the list of a tangible hospitality thank you.

    A. Manicure. Pedicure, facial or massage at a nifty spa

    B. Dinner for two at a really nice restaurant

      C. Local sporting goods store

      D. Local handyman store such as *Home Depot or Lowes.*

      E. Local book store such as Barnes and Nobel or Borders or some local book boutique.

      F. Local stationery store.

      G. Upscale cookware from a kitchen store such as *Sonoma Williams*

      H. The local bird center

      I. The local garden center

II. Tickets

      A. Local theater

      B. Game tickets, baseball, football, basketball, tennis.

III. If the host's reading appetites are known, an appropriate book would be timely. So would a magazine subscription that moves with the host/ess interests. Go to the local drugstore and buy a magazine that fits the interest of your host family, tear out the subscription leaflet. Send it in with your remittance before leaving the host premises. At the end of the visit, give the host the magazine along with a gift card explaining that they will soon receive the magazine.

Some suggestions follow:

      A. Field and Stream

      B. Photography

    C. Women's magazines

    D. Cooking magazines

    E. Children's magazines

IV. For the home

    A. A set of lovely new bath towels

    B. A nifty birdhouse or feeder

    C. Placemats and napkins

    D. A lovely piece of crystal

    E. A pair of a <u>quality</u> garden gloves and clippers (for gardeners)

    F. A bottle of fine liquor for those who have a discerning liquor cabinet. (For those guests who are drinkers, bring along a bottle of your favorite drink: vodka, gin, scotch, bourbon or wine in addition to the houseguest gift.

Note: It is almost always appropriate for the guests to appear at the door with a <u>very</u> fine bottle of wine. Bringing a bottle of $2.00 wine simply isn't done –ever!

    G. A basket of home-grown fruits is appropriate and usually well received.

Many of you will come up with great ideas of your own. Do pass these ideas along to darlenedennis@hostorhostage.com.

If you really want to make an enemy, think of something tasteless or hurtful including:

1. A scale and or a book on dieting along with fat-free and sugar-free foods for a host that looks or seems to be overweight.

2. Nicotine patches for smokers.

3. The Alcoholics anonymous Big Book for drinkers.

4. Anything of a tasteless nature such as a bathroom book or anything pornographic.

The guest makes a point of treating the host family to a dinner out at a nice restaurant during the visit. Recently, however, we had the unnerving experience of being treated to dinner by a guest. When the bill arrived, his credit card was returned to him because his balance was deficient to cover the bill. Embarrassed, his wife shuffled around and came up with her credit card. Yup, this is Boorish Bob, the same drinker, snorer, critic, arguer, dallier and "know-it–all," alluded to throughout this book. By the way, he left us a gift of a home made candle.

Most of us have committed social blunders Embarrassment is certainly a normal reaction to the realization of one's own inappropriate behavior. If possible, apologize to the offended person when the boundaries of taste have been violated. Hopefully, we then need to learn from the experience and move on to a more poised demeanor.

Notice how politicians fumble for an excuse when behavior overreaches acceptable boundaries. They aren't alone. It has been said that to err is human and to forgive, divine, but a host who feels his hospitality has been violated is apt to have his divine spark extinguished. Guests who flail around for usually unacceptable excuses to cover their excesses are apt to be labeled "adolescent" evermore. The dog may have eaten the airline ticket requiring them to add additional time to their already overlong stay, but it is doubtful that a host in his right mind will be very forgiving. Some really unforgivable guest behaviors to avoid that may well imperil the next vacation include the following:

1. Arriving before the designated invitation time

2. Extending the visit beyond the designated invitation departure date.

3. Dallying at the door. It's been a great visit, but don't linger– even if the host seems insistent that you stay. They may well be tired of you in spite of protests to the contrary. The host family needs its time territory and space restored.

4. Asking to borrow or use the host's car.

5. Arriving without enough money to cover your personal expenses, to purchase any special food you may require while visiting, admission to tourist attractions or to take the host family out for a nice dinner.

6. Leaving personal belongings in the community areas of the house: medications, shoes, books.

7. Assuming that the computer or telephone is at the guest's disposal without first asking.

8. Taking ownership of the television remote control. Please note: this is usually the lone territory of the elder male member of the household. However, if there is no male head of household, the female claims ownership. Folks are, more often than not, really picky about their television preferences.

9. Talking on a cell phone in the presence of others.

10. Talking on the cell phone during any meal.

11. Tying up the host's phone line with your computer. (Don't even ask. If you need to use a computer, go to a local computer outlet to do your business).

12. Poor to bad table manners including:

    A. Talking with mouth full.

    B. Reaching in front of others to access food or other items on the table.

    C. Starting to eat before everyone has been served.

    D. Picking up food from a communal plate with fingers and then putting it back.

    E. Putting a knife in one's mouth to lap it off.

13. Several conversational no-no's including:

    A. Interrupting

    B. Hogging the conversation

    C. Engaging in topics only interesting to the talker,

    D. Chronically contradicting every issue

    E. Not talking at all.

    F. Overstating the obvious and then talking it to death.

G. Initiating conversation on politics, religion or lengthy diatribes on one's children or grandchildren

H. Pouting

14. Arriving at the host's home with an uninvited other adult, child or pet

15. Arriving without being invited

16. Using bed clothes for anything other than their intended use as bed coverings

17. Breaking anything without repairing, replacing or paying for its replacement

18. Thoughtless loud noise whether it be music (not of the host's choice) snoring, arguing, noisy sex, or too loud voices

19. Refusing to join in on planned activities

20. If you happen to be a smoker, don't embarrass yourself by asking if it is alright to smoke. It isn't!

21. Failure to bring, at least a token gift for the host

22. Not emptying waste baskets in the assigned area

23. Not emptying waste can—especially if it is filled with dirty diapers

24. Failure to bring the appropriate attire (clothes selections) for the planned events during the visit

25. Not taking care of and cleaning up after one's own children or pets if they are included in the guest list

26. Dying your hair in the host's bathroom. Bathroom floors and sinks damaged by hair dye is beyond regrettable. The damage needs to be acknowledged and paid for by the offending guest.

27. Re-arranging the host's furniture, cupboards, or providing unsolicited décor to the living quarters

28. Looking in drawers, cupboards, closets, filing cabinets, or computer files belonging exclusively to the host and not assigned to the guests

29. Failure to treat family members and guests of the host with friendliness and respect.

30. Cluttering the house with personal belongings

31. Leaving behind belongings upon your departure. The host family has a life after your visit. Hunting down, packing up and mailing your jewelry, sunglasses, umbrella, or hiking boots is beyond inconvenient. Be thorough about checking the territory where you slept, bathed, etc.

32. Treating the host's home as though it is a hotel

33. Expecting the host to provide all and do all

"By the pricking of my thumbs, something wicked this way comes." Is the line that Shakespeare put into the mouth of the witch who predicted that Macbeth was destined to play the role of the "wicked one" (In this case the host) who murdered King Duncan, his guest. In reverse, there may be guests who are murderous to entertain. By the time they finally leave, the soul is drained — not to mention the household resources. Violating unwritten rules — whether knowingly and deliberately or not— creates discomfort among those who conform. These transgressors are fodder for self-help columnists and the precipitating factor in the initiation and completion of this book. Like the person who enters an elevator and faces the back wall, those surrounding conformists, facing the door, will be uneasy with the violation of a tacit rule. When these insensitive overstepping irritants finally roll away, harried hosts are bidding them "good riddance!" It was Oscar Wilde who said, "Some cause happiness wherever they go; others, whenever they go."

Those who have been heavenly house guests will surely be hailed farewell with a request to return or plans to meet again. It will require both host and guest to exercise the mutual obligations that create a comfortable and mutually satisfying experience.

Finally: A Note of Thanks

The host family has opened the doors to their home so you could vacate yours and experience some time with them in their part of the state, country or world. Their generosity in setting aside time, territory, privacy and provisions to entertain you, necessitates a thank you note. No, an e-mail "thank you" won't do. Go out and purchase a pretty card and in your best <u>cursive</u> handwriting done in blue or black ink, thank the host family for all they have done. Be sure and mention outstanding highlights of the visit. Describe an activity that you enjoyed together even if it was an evening of warm conversation. Be sure to compliment the food and/or accommodations. If your children have been part of the visit, be sure and have them write their own notes along with yours. You want to leave your hosts with your warmest thanks for their hospitality and your pleasurable recollections of the visit.

Printed in the United States
150477LV00003B/3/P